the illustrated

Koka Shastra

the illustrated

Koka Shastra

Medieval Indian Writings on Love

Based on the Kama Sutra

Translated and with introduction by

ALEX COMFORT, M.B., D.SC.

Preface by W. G. ARCHER

Consultant Editor CHARLES FOWKES

SIMON & SCHUSTER EDITIONS
Rockefeller Center
1230 Avenue of the Americas
New York, NY 10020

Copyright © 1997 by Reed International Books Limited

Text copyright © 1966, 1997 by Alex Comfort

This edition published in 1997 by
SIMON & SCHUSTER EDITIONS,
by arrangement with Mitchell Beazley, an
imprint of Reed International Books Limited,
Michelin House, 81 Fulham Road,
London, SW3 6RB England

SIMON & SCHUSTER EDITIONS and colophon are
trademarks of Simon & Schuster Inc.

Designed by Simon Balley and David McCourt

Manufactured in Hong Kong by Mandarin Offset

1 2 3 4 5 6 7 8 9 10

Library of Congress Cataloging-in-Publication
data is available

ISBN 0-684-83981-4

Warning:
The texts contained in this book are translations of
medieval Indian erotic texts. The publisher and the
translator, Dr Alex Comfort, would like to stress that in
no way do they endorse or advocate the use of these texts
for practical purposes or instruction and they cannot
accept any legal responsibility or liability for any personal
injury caused as a result of such use. No guarantee of any
kind is given as to the safety or health of any practice
described in the book and the texts should be read in the
light of present understanding of health risks
from sexually transmitted diseases.

Note on pronunciation:
In transliteration of Sanskrit names and
words c = English "ch" as in chin,
and s = English "sh" as in ship;
r when used as a vowel is pronounced rri
(i.e., mrgi is pronounced approximately mrrigi).

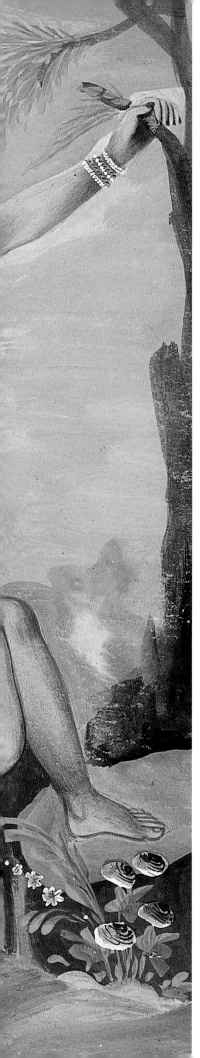

CONTENTS

Preface *by W. G. Archer*

In 1882 Sir Richard Burton and F. F. Arbuthnot founded in London the Kama Shastra Society. Its purpose was to publish "the Hindu erotic"; and among the first texts it issued was a medieval Indian classic, the Ananga Ranga or "Stage of the Love-God." The book was written in the sixteenth century by an Indian poet, Kalyan Mall, and was a subtle and detailed treatise on love and sex. During the years 1868 to 1879—the period when Arbuthnot worked in Bombay as a senior Indian civil servant—this book was still one of the most popular with Indians and, as a means of enlightening the British public on Indian sex, it seemed to Arbuthnot an obvious choice for translation. Burton agreed, and in about 1869 Arbuthnot set to work. He employed Indian pundits or scholars, and while translating with them, he found two intriguing references. These named a certain Vatsya as chief authority and respectfully cited his ancient book. In 1872 Arbuthnot went on furlough, but on his return to India in 1874 a quest for

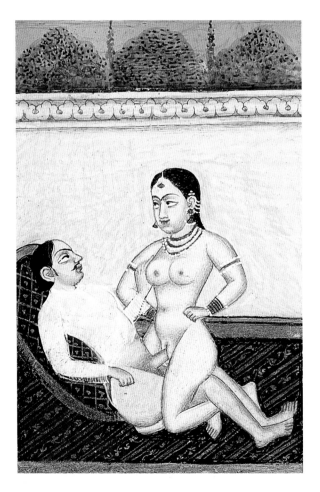

Vatsya's classic began. "No Sanskrit library was supposed to be complete without a copy," and although the search was far longer than this claim suggests, at last the book was found. It was the Kama Sutra of about the third century A.D.—the earliest and most profound discussion of love and sex written in India. Once more Arbuthnot sat with pundits. He made a translation, and his version, improved and given style by Burton, was the first text to be published by the new society.

Arbuthnot's work did not end here. From the ancient, he turned to the medieval, and the result was the discovery of a whole series of Indian writings on sex. The latest in date was the Ananga Ranga. The earliest was the Ratirahasya, "The secrets of Rati, spouse of the Love-God." It was known as the Koka Shastra—"the scripture of Koka"—and had been composed in the twelfth century by a poet named Kokkoka. Like the Ananga Ranga, the Koka Shastra discussed sexual positions in detail, forms of love-play, and ways of satisfying a woman's passions.

Burton and Arbuthnot did not translate the Koka Shastra. They came across the text as part of their study of Indian life and were content merely to list this book along with other erotic texts. They did not ask what attitudes the Koka Shastra texts expressed, how they differed from the Kama Sutra, or how they fitted into an Indian tradition. As translators, the main concerns of Burton and Arbuthnot lay elsewhere. In a footnote to Ananga Ranga's definition of the woman who can most easily be subdued—"she who has never learned the real delight of carnal copulation"—they wrote "which allow us to state is the case with most English women and a case to be remedied by constant and intelligent study of the Ananga Ranga scripture." Worthy as it is, the footnote is also a reminder that the Victorian translators (in common with the ancient authors) were men writing for men.

The German scholar, Richard Schmidt, was the first to translate and analyze the other erotic texts that Burton and Arbuthnot had discovered. The Koka Shastra had to wait until 1964 for an English translation, and appropriately the

◁ *A woman clad in jewels rides upon her lover in a purusayita or inverse position.*

▷ *Kama, the Love-God, proudly atop his sacred mare of beautiful adoring women.*

doctor who had the initiative to produce it is also—like the book's original author—a poet. The delay can hardly have been more fortunate since in Dr. Alex Comfort's version, the Koka Shastra obtains the sensitive treatment it requires. Not only does Dr. Comfort render the original with discerning skill, but his delicate and lively English communicates the subtle poetry of the original. His version continues the pioneer work on Indian culture begun by Burton and Arbuthnot and enables the reader to assess for the first time the importance of this classic text.

Sex Ancient and Medieval

Medieval India is not ancient India. The Koka Shastra is not the Kama Sutra. Any discussion of the Koka Shastra must begin with these two statements, for only then can we grasp the true significance of this book.

The Kama Sutra was put together around the third century A.D. The author, Vatsyayana, did not claim to be original—he summed up existing wisdom. His book had authority, and for almost a thousand years no one else wrote anything like it. It was the classic treatise on Indian love and sex.

In the twelfth century, the poet Kokkoka decided to look again at the Kama Sutra—a bold move which, in a sense, determined his treatment of the Koka Shastra. Indian life was no longer what it had been. A new approach was needed, yet the early pages of the Koka Shastra suggest that we are reading an abridgement of the Kama Sutra, a sibling rather than a sequel. Like the author of the Ananga Ranga, Kokkoka refers with nostalgic reverence to "the Founder of Our Science." He looks back to Vatsyayana (the author of the Kama Sutra) much as the Renaissance looked back to ancient Greece.

Though he is facing new conditions in India, Kokkoka can never quite rid himself of the feeling that Vatsyayana had expressed the ultimate wisdom—that he had said almost, if not quite, the last word. We find him, therefore, giving an account of his master's principles, distinguishing those which are Vatsyayana's own from those of two other authors on whom Vatsyayana had drawn. Only then can he move to his proper subject—love and sex in his own time. "This work," he explains, "was composed by one Kokkoka, poet, as a light to satisfy the curiosity of the Most Excellent Vainyadatta concerning the art of love." And he concludes: "With zeal was this book written by Kokkoka for the greater enjoyment of all lovers." The questions we must ask are: Who were these lovers? How did they regard the Koka Shastra? What part did Kokkoka's book play in medieval India?

Kokkoka's lovers were obviously very different from those of Vatsyayana. The ancient India of the Kama Sutra was relatively carefree and happy. It was like tribal society in modern India—Santal, Uraon, and Naga. Men were dominant, but women moved freely in public and were not secluded. Girls were courted by young men. Marriage was normal, sometimes on a plural basis. Premarital love was common. So, too, was extramarital sex. Courtesans were greatly admired, but other women also had sexual adventures. Vatsyayana thought it worthwhile to discuss these sexual adventures at some length, and it is worth noting how very few kinds of women were really excluded. Only with women of castes higher than the man's own or with those of the same caste but who had previously been enjoyed by others, was sex strictly forbidden. Certain others, he said, were "not to be enjoyed," but perhaps more in the sense that he strongly advised against it than an absolute "no." Some were barred on grounds of hygiene and esthetics—a leper, a bad-smelling woman, a lunatic, a woman who was either over-white or over-black. Others were barred for defects of character—a woman turned out of her caste, one who reveals secrets, one who is so blatantly wanton that she "publicly expresses desire for sexual intercourse." With some, such as near relations and "female friends"—girls with whom the man had grown up as a child—sex might well be socially too embarrassing. In a similar way, a woman who led the life of an ascetic was also to be avoided—perhaps because her mode of life gave her magical charms and sex with her would therefore be dangerous. But apart from these, and always excepting a special code for adultery, sex in ancient India was extraordinarily free.

An Ordered Universe

Vaharamihira—who composed the Brihat Samhita or Complete System of Natural Astrology in the sixth century A. D.—gives a wonderful if fantastic description of what contemporary life was like. It was ruled, he believed, by planets, stars, moon, and sun, and it was these that accounted for annual variations. Yet the basic pattern was remarkably constant.

In the course of a year ruled by the Moon, the sky is covered with clouds that, showing the dark hue of snakes, collyrium and, buffalo's horn, and resembling mountains in motion, fill the whole earth with pure water and the air with a deep sound such as arouses a feeling of tender longing. The lakes are decked with lotuses and water lilies, the trees are blossoming, and the bees humming in the parks; the cows yield abundant milk; lovers unceasingly delight their delightful paramours by amorous sports; the sovereigns rule an earth rich in flourishing towns and mines, in wheat, rice, barley, and fields of sugarcane, while she is dotted with fire-piles and resounding with the noise of greater and smaller sacrifices.

In a year ruled by the planet Venus, earth is decked with rice and sugarcane, for the fields are copiously watered by the rain poured from mountainlike clouds; by her numerous tanks adorned with beautiful lotuses, she shines like a woman brilliant with new ornaments. The rulers of the country destroy their powerful enemies. The good rejoice and the wicked are put down. At springtime there is much sipping of sweet wine in company with dear loves, much delightful singing accompanied by flute and lute, much feasting in company with guests, friends, and kinsfolk, and Love's shouts of triumph are ringing in a year ruled by Venus.

This account is reminiscent of the descriptions of ancient Rome under the emperors. There is the same prevalence of overlapping codes—a code for marriage, a code for sex outside marriage, and at all points there is a cult of intensity in both love and sex.

Adultery and Passion

Ancient India and ancient Rome were strangely alike in their views of adultery. Roman society took adultery for granted, and no attempt was made to square it with Roman ethics or religion. This was how Romans behaved. Vatsyayana had much the same approach. Adultery was a fact in ancient India. It was one of many modes of loving, and although he had several reservations, he discussed it with rational calm. It should never, he thought, be lightly undertaken, and with wives of relations, Brahmins, and Kings, it must definitely be avoided. Yet certain circumstances presented no difficulties. If adultery might lead the woman to influence her husband and if, for business or other reasons, the lover needed to influence the husband, it was the obvious thing to do. At least thirteen such circumstances existed, and Vatsyayana explained all of them with patient care. "For these and similar other reasons," he said, "the wives of other men may be resorted to."

Seductions of this kind were nothing if not calculated. Indeed, there is a sense in which Vatsyayana is rational almost to the point of chilly detachment. Yet even as he pleads for a logical approach, he abandons it. He sees that passionate, frantic desire may override prudence. In such circumstances, intensity was the deciding factor. When "passion love" was so great that the lover was beside himself with longing, nothing short of adultery might save his life. As a man perceived that

▲ *"At springtime there is much sipping of sweet wine"—a lovers' picnic reaches its inevitable conclusion.*

his love for a married woman was moving from one degree of intensity to another, from love of the eye to attachment of the mind, and then on to "constant reflection, destruction of sleep, emaciation of the body, turning away from objects of enjoyment, removal of shame, madness, fainting, and finally death"—in such circumstances, there was no alternative.

"Love and death," "a fatal love"—these phrases sum up the sentiment of popular poems, whatever is universally appealing in Western literature and art from the oldest legends to the latest songs. Happy love has no history. Romance only comes into existence where love is fatal and doomed by life itself. What stirs lyrical poets to their finest flights is neither the delight of the senses nor the fruitful contentment of the settled couple; not the satisfaction of love, but its passion. And passion means suffering. There we have the fundamental fact.

Everything within and about us glorifies passion: our yearning for both novels and films that contain struggle and heartbreak; the idealized eroticism that we see all around us providing the pictures that fill the background of our lives: our desire for "escape," made worse by a mechanical boredom. In some ways the prospect of a passionate experience could imply that we are about to live more full and more intense lives. We look upon passion as a transfiguring force, something beyond delight and pain. In "passion" we are not aware of that "which suffers," only of what is "thrilling." And yet passionate love is a misfortune. In this respect, manners have undergone no change for many centuries, and the community still drives passionate love in nine cases out of ten to take the form of adultery. No doubt lovers call upon numerous exceptions. But the statistics state otherwise.

Love and Death

In ancient India, love and death were equally intermixed. But the approach was the complete reverse. Adultery might cause unhappiness, yet, equally, unhappiness might permit adultery. Adulterous love was "fatal"—but only when it was repressed. In practice, therefore, Vatsyayana made large concessions. A man or woman had only to fall in love—to be gripped by an overwhelming passion—for their situation to become "fatal." When that happened, all controls and restraints were suspended. Indeed, there is a strange contrast between the Vatsyayana who counsels prudence and the author who faces life as it is. Life in ancient India had its own rationale: more concerned with living than with thinking. Practice overrode precept, and as a result, a number of pages in the Kama Sutra discuss in detail how best to seduce a married woman—once the feverish passion is on.

It is clear that certain married women were ready to be seduced and the lover had only to follow some obvious rules in order to achieve success. In the Kama Sutra, Vatsyayana, in fact, returns again and again to love and sex as something amoral, something which transcends ethics and has its own justifications. He observed: "A wise man having regard to his reputation should not think of seducing a woman who is apprehensive, timid, not to be trusted, well guarded, or possessed of a father-in-law and mother-in-law." But the implication is plain. Provided the married woman is not handicapped in any of these ways, the lover should bring the affair to its logical conclusion. Then, he calmly sums up,

"Desire, which springs from nature, and which is increased by art and from which all danger is taken away by wisdom, becomes firm and secure. A clever man, depending on his own ability and observing carefully the ideas and thoughts of women and removing the causes of their turning away from men, is generally successful with them."

Such a philosophy of love and sex—which might almost be defined as rapturous opportunism—was part of ancient India. But it is important to understand that it in no way conflicted with, or contradicted religion. Religion or dharma was not based upon communion with God. It was rather a form of public conduct, a set of rites, a series of festivals, a code of offerings and sacrifices. It was these that constituted "merit." Life itself was a long series of births and rebirths, and whether under Buddhism or Brahmanical Hinduism, the ultimate goal was release from living through integration with God. This was rarely achieved at once. Each life brought an individual nearer to or farther from the goal. What you did in one life affected where you started in the next. By living correctly, by scrupulously observing the proper rites, you gained a better position in your next rebirth. In that way the individual moved by gradual stages towards ultimate release. This system, known as samsara (literally "passing through"), was the remorseless machinery governing all human existence. Living correctly, however, and this is the crucial point—did not exclude loving. It applied rather to aspects of life other than sex. It meant avoiding "sin." But "sin" was more a breach of purity than of ethics. Only if sex involved "pollution" was it "sin." Such "sin" could be cancelled by deeds of "merit" and if, despite all lapses, your stock of "merit" was large, you could still be promoted to a higher stage in your next life.

An Erotic Paradise

In certain circumstances an individual could even earn a spell in heaven, a temporary reward for following dharma* successfully in a former life. In his book *Sexual Life in Ancient India*, J. J. Meyer describes the kind of heaven a warrior of the period expected: "intercourse with thousands of lovely women in the bloom of youth, smiling with long lotus-eyes at the man, winding their rounded arms about his neck and pressing their swelling firm breasts against him—women who press their great swelling hips and thighs like banana-stems against his body, who give lips red as the bimbafruit to be sucked by his and as they glow in the act of sex not only

★ In Hinduism, darma is the duty to follow law and custom.

▲ *The practice of painting on ivory allowed Indian
miniaturists to achieve luminous flesh tones.*

receive but also give." Heaven in those contemporary male fantasies seems to be inhabited by celestial glamour-girls, and they are not merely enjoyed in heaven but can sometimes be called to earth.

The Ramayana, the second of the great Hindu epics, which was written around 300 B.C., includes a vivid passage translated by Meyer which describes how a rishi or holy man greets the army of Bharata as it goes to fetch the banished Rama. "From out of India's paradise he called down the whole host of the apsarases and from other heavens other divine women. Twenty thousand of these wondrous beauties were sent by Brahma, twenty thousand by Kubera, twenty thousand by Indra, even the creepers in the forest did the yogi turn into delightful women. Seven or eight of these charming examples of ravishing womanhood gave each warrior, mostly married, their service for the bath and offered him heady drink and the flower-cups of their divine bodies." Nothing in fact could better illustrate the basic attitudes of ancient India. Not merely is sex one thing and religion another. In certain circumstances love and sex are actual rewards for "religious" living.

▲ *Indian artists often used intertwined lovers to make elaborate visual jokes.*

Husbands and Wives

Medieval India stood in sharp contrast to this contented and sensuous regime. The goal of life was still the same. It was a final breaking-out from a chain of births and rebirths. But the terms of living were now much harsher. Rigid principles had been outlined. Morals were tighter. Male dominance had become more marked. There was more tension.

The first sphere in which a new severity appears is that of marriage. A medieval text, the Brahma Vaivarta Purana, is in no doubt as to the role of a wife.

A chaste woman serves her husband, the source of her own dignity. To a chaste woman, the husband is a friend and a god. She is helpless without him. He represents all her prosperity. The husband, the source of her virtue, happiness, contentment, tranquility, and honor can solely appease her jealousy and elevate her to dignity. Of all substantial things in the world prized by a woman, the husband is the best. He is the best of her friends. He maintains her, preserves her, gives her material prosperity, is lord of her life, enjoys her. There is none dearer than the husband to a woman. A son is dear to her, as he is the offspring of her husband. The husband is dearer to a woman than a hundred sons. A wicked woman who does not know the merits of her husband adopts the evil path. Ablution in all holy waters, initiation in all ceremonies, asceticism, vows and gifts of all kinds, fasts, worship of the preceptor or the gods, and other difficult rites are not equal in point of merit to a sixteenth part of the devotion of a woman to her husband

It follows that chastity is a woman's supreme virtue, and the authors of the Brahma Vaivarta Purana do not merely denounce an unchaste woman but load a chaste woman with exaggerated praises. Their words strike a puritanical note that might almost be Milton's:

> So dear to Heaven is saintly chastity,
> That when a soul is found sincerely so
> A thousand liveried angels lacky her,
> Driving far off each thing of sin and guilt,
> And in clear dream and solemn vision
> Tell her of things that no gross ear can hear

It isn't surprising that, in such a society, adultery should be denounced as the most heinous of offenses. Not only does it defy the ideal but, in keeping with the ever-increasing importance attached to "purity," it flouts society in its most sensitive sphere. It insults the husband's position, and it ceremonially pollutes him, and for these reasons, it carries terrible penalties. And the text makes this very clear.

Whoever enjoys the society of a woman courted by another man dwells in the hell called the thread of time so long as the sun and the moon exist. A vile woman is not fit for an act sacred to the manes or the gods. The husband loses his grace and valor by embracing her. Brahma himself has said that oblations to fire or offerings of water made by such a man do not satisfy the gods or the manes. That is why learned men carefully preserve their wives; otherwise they are consigned to hell. A wife and a cooking vessel should always be carefully preserved; for they are consecrated by the touch of others. A woman who defrauds her husband and courts another lover is consigned to hell as long as the sun and the moon exist. The myrmidons of Yama (the god of death) chastise her if, afflicted with tortures, she tries to run away. In hell she is bitten by worms as big as snakes. The bite causes her to scream in pain but does not affect her life. For the sake of pleasure, which only lasts for a few minutes, the wretch forfeits fair fame in this world and is consigned to hell hereafter. Therefore the virtuous try their best to shield their wives from the gaze of others. In a word, the woman is blessed who is not touched even by the sun's rays. A vile woman who is independent of the control of her husband resembles a sow in all her features.

No writer in ancient India would have expressed so complete a repugnance or done it in such a virulent manner.

Crime and Punishment

Yet if women must be moral so also should men and, in the medieval conception of religion, human virtues were sometimes those of God himself. By the sixth century, God was being thought of as the Hindu Trinity. This comprised Brahma the Creator, Vishnu the loving Preserver, and Siva the Procreator and Destroyer. It was by directly approaching Vishnu and Siva that a man not only lived a better life but life itself was better. Before the Indian Middle Ages, Vishnu had had nine incarnations. His early incarnations do not concern us, but his seventh, Rama, is the equivalent in religion of the very moralistic code just discussed. Rama embodies virtue. He is moral. He observes the rules of dharma. He is a model king with a model consort, Sita. When Sita is abducted by a demon, he searches for her until he finds her. But morality must be seen to be respected. Although Sita was abducted, she has in fact preserved her chastity. Rama's subjects cannot believe this for the very situation had in their eyes made chastity impossible. In compliance to the new morality,

Rama therefore discards Sita—disregarding human "goodness" but powerfully reinforcing the current ideals of marriage and chastity. In the form of Rama, the "moral man," Vishnu appealed to much of medieval India: his worship involved not only love of God but love of morals.

So blatant a denial of the senses provoked its own reaction. When rigid fixity informs society, when sex is viewed with disapproval except when strictly moral, the very fact of repression engenders revolt. In medieval India, religion itself developed certain cults and sects as if in compensation. In these cults, passionate abandonment was given direct expression, and sex received mystical and symbolic interpretations.

Divine Lovers

A first sign of this contrary tendency is the cult of Krishna, the divine lover, literally "the dark-colored one." Following Rama, Krishna had been born as Vishnu's eighth incarnation.

This elaborate wood carving depicts an adulterous woman with Yama, the god of death.

His purpose was to slay demons and encourage the righteous. He was born a prince (indeed, some believe he was an historical figure) and brought up, not in princely circles, but among cowherds. During his brief idyllic youth, he made love to all the young married women. He also ridiculed offerings and sacrifices, humbled Indra, the conventional lord of the gods, and outwitted the city Brahmins (or official priesthood) of Mathura by inducing their wives to meet him against their husbands' wishes. Among the cowgirls he had a special love, Radha, and his love for her and the other cowgirls involved the very "crime" denounced in the Brahma Vaivarta Purana. Indeed, this religious text, in the face of such a defiant breach of medieval morals, endeavors to persuade the reader that Krishna's love for Radha was not at all adulterous—that from eternity they have in fact been married. Its special pleading is totally unconvincing.

The whole meaning of Krishna's romance with Radha is that it places love before duty. Vishnu as Krishna brings a new element into Indian religion—an element which goes to the opposite extreme from that of Rama, the "moral man." Love, from being outside religion, is made its crux. Love of Krishna or Vishnu—enraptured devotion to the holy character and name—could win the devotee immediate "release." It short-circuited the laborious process of births and rebirths, the painful climbing from one level to the next. It was an act of grace, a grant of salvation, a divine reward not for correct living but for love and adoration.

Such love was not itself sexual love, but sexual love is the closest to it. In the sixth century, Krishna's story was included in the Vishnu Purana, but its full meaning was suppressed. In the tenth century, it was told in greater detail in the Bhagavata Purana and, although Radha's name was omitted, Krishna's sexual raptures with the cowgirls were mentioned. It is only in the twelfth century—at the time when Kokkoka was writing his book of poems—that the hidden meaning in the story was given clear expression. The Sanskrit poet, Jayadeva, not only mentions Radha, but makes her romance with Krishna the very heart of his great poem, the Gita-Govinda. Their love is strongly sexual, but the relationship is viewed in mystical terms. Radha in adoring Krishna is compared to the soul adoring God. Adoration is the supreme type of "merit." In sexual rapture, there is a sense of losing one's self and this is a symbol of losing oneself in God. To love God was not only a mystical experience but a salvation. While medieval India was pressing romantic love out of life, Indian religion was contemplating adultery.

"Lord of Time and Death"

The same "annexation" of sex by religion is reflected in the worship of Siva. In contrast to the mild and benign Vishnu (see p.13), Siva was thought of as a strange erratic being, full of moods and furies, responsible for what was sudden and unexpected, a destroyer but also a procreator. His worship, like Vishnu's, involved daily prayers, but these were to avert disaster and obtain favors rather than to save. It was difficult to adore Siva, but you could model your life on his wild ascetic practices and humor his tantrums.

Siva's idol was a phallus or lingam set in the yoni or female organ, and the very starkness of the symbol gave sex a new significance. It was by adoring the lingam that childless women sometimes became pregnant and men themselves obtained insight. Besides the cult of Siva, other cults resorted to sexual symbolism. The secret force behind the universe was sometimes regarded as female, even as maternal, and, in the cult of shakti, women became a sacred object, an incarnation of the Mother. Sensual ecstasy was also identified with "annihilation," and among certain sub-cults of Siva, intensity was the key to worship. These cults were organized as secret societies. They involved acts of sex, and their prevalence proves how far medieval India had traveled from the carefree state of ancient India.

Shrine to Sexuality

This erotic upsurgence was reflected in medieval temples and sculptures. Temples were usually reserved for Vishnu himself or for Siva. Each resembled a palace in which, attended by gods and dancing girls, Vishnu and Siva held majestic court. Sculpture contributed to this effect. Ascending the temple facade in row upon row, sculptures of the gods mingled with bands of glamour-girls—each girl with her slim vertical form reinforcing the feeling of exaltation induced by the upward sweep of the building itself, while her sexual charm hinted at the rapturous nature of union with God. This erotic element was, at times, taken still further, and lovers were sculpted in the act of union. Their poses, as Dr. Comfort has pointed out, seldom tally with any of those described by either Vatsyayana or Kokkoka, and we can perhaps explain them on only two hypotheses. Their strange acrobatics, their very impossibility—in a temple at Khajuraho the lover is even standing on his head—gives them an air of ideal fantasy. It is as if the artificial and extravagant have acquired a special value, as if only through the unknown and the unusual can sexual frenzy be fully conveyed. Just as a period of nervous strain, of cultural malaise, may well have prefigured the Mannerist movement in Western art, strain in medieval India may also have evoked the same kind of fevered sexuality.

A second viewpoint would regard all standing lovers as in fact lying flat, yet shown, for purposes of architecture, as upright. Supine or horizontal designs and compositions would detract from the upward movement of the temple. They would be appropriate in "feminine" buildings such as the Jefferson Memorial in Washington D.C., or the National Gallery in London—buildings whose flat lines support a rounded breast-like dome and whose masculine counterpart are such structures as the Washington Monument or Nelson's column. Temples in medieval India were male in their own right. Their towers were like lingams. As sculpture, then, the lovers' vertical positions are geared to this conception. But lay them down, make the necessary mental adjustment and what is wild and fantastic is once again conventional.

Such sculptures may well have had two roles. If in ancient India sex was regarded as inherently noble, sexual rapture was the most compelling analogy for spiritual bliss. It showed what Indian religion was about. "In the embrace of his beloved, a man forgets the whole world—everything both within and without; in the same way he who embraces the Self knows neither within nor without." The words are from an ancient text, the Brhadaranyaka Upanishad, but they sum up a whole way of Indian thought. In medieval India, the maithuna—a sculpture of a sexual embrace, a loving couple—has a sexual function. Here is sex pursued with daring abandonment, sex that in its freedom appears to exemplify romance and passion. What is condemned in real life is countenanced in sculpture and religion.

Middle Ages—Middle Class

It was for such a society that the erotic books of medieval India, the Koka Shastra and the Ananga Ranga, were written. They mirrored life as it had now become, and both in character and in attitude their "lovers" are quite new. For ardent seducers and roving adventurers, there was now little scope. Men and women no longer met socially. Premarital courtship had gone out. Woman's place was in the home and there she was constantly watched. As a younger girl, a child, she was married before she reached puberty. Romance had been banished and in its place had come an even sharper stress on wifely duty. For the very powerful or the very rich, variety in sex might still be possible. But it was obtained more by marrying a great many wives, installing concubines or hiring

▲ *Hanuman, the mischievous monkey-god, pays his respects to Rama, divine embodiment of sexual morality and chastity.*

dancing-girls and prostitutes than by free adventure. At Mandu in Central India in the fifteenth century, a Khilji ruler created a whole "city of women" by marshalling 15,000 women at his court. Later, in the sixteenth century, his Pathan successor, Prince Baz Bahadur, fell in love with a Hindu courtesan, Rupmati. Their romance was as free as in ancient India—the two lovers riding together at night and gazing into each other's eyes. Such a romance, however, was so unusual that it later took on a legendary glamour. From the eighteenth century onward, Baz Bahadur and Rupmati were portrayed in Indian painting as vivid exemplars of romance, as rivals in real life to lovers in poetry. Only a relationship that cut right across accepted conduct could have evoked such

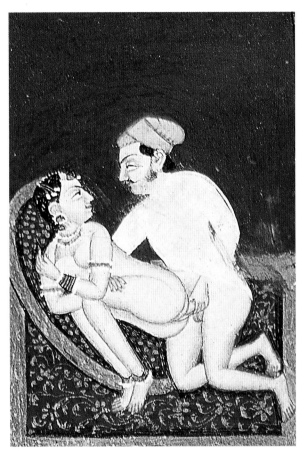

▲ *In the coital posture known as vyanata, in union the couple imitates different animals.*

frequent or such fervent celebration. In medieval India as a whole, quite other norms prevailed. This makes for a surprising position. In both the Koka Shastra and the Ananga Ranga, the lover of ancient India has almost ceased to exist. The men for whom these two books were written were certainly not lovers but husbands.

This purpose is stated forcefully in the Ananga Ranga. "No one yet has written a book to prevent the separation of the married pair and to show them how they may pass through life in union. Seeing this (its author writes), I felt compassion and composed the treatise." Sex outside marriage was disastrous and in order to combat its chief cause—"the want of varied pleasures" and "the monotony which follows possession"—he explains how "the husband, by varying the enjoyment of his wife, may live with her as with thirty-two different women, ever varying the enjoyment of her and rendering satiety impossible." He concludes: "If husband and wife live together in close agreement, as one soul in a single body, they shall be happy in this world, and in that to come.

Their good and charitable actions will be an example to mankind and their peace and harmony will effect their salvation." He then lists all the factors on which sex in marriage depends, urging again and again that woman's need for "carnal enjoyment" is paramount and that only if the woman is satisfied can the husband be pleased. The Ananga Ranga is a marriage manual, not a lover's handbook.

Love and Marriage

Yet the poet-author of the Ananga Ranga was clearly faced with a strange predicament. Romance might be rare and even dangerous to marriage, but society needed to believe that it could happen. It was to assure medieval India that love could still exist that the author evolved a compromise. Adhering to marriage as the one true goal, he revived the more romantic part of the Kama Sutra but with a difference. Following Vatsyayana, he describes what kinds of women lend themselves most readily to seduction, how go-betweens can help, and where intrigues should be carried on. He describes, but at the same time, he cautions. He minimizes chances. He magnifies what is forbidden. Even his manner is different. Where the Kama Sutra is calm and objective, the Ananga Ranga at times resembles the Brahma Vaivarta Purana in its stern condemnation. "The following women are absolutely and under all circumstances to be excluded from commerce. The wife of a Brahmin, of a Brahmin learned in the Vedas, of a priest who keeps up the sacred fire, and of a Puranik (reader of the Puranas). To look significantly at such a woman, or to think of her with a view to sensual desire, is highly improper: what then, must we think of the sin of carnal copulation with her? In like manner men prepare to go to hell by lying with the wife of a king or any man of the warrior caste; of a friend or of a relation. The author of the book strongly warns and commands his readers to avoid all such deadly sins." Finally he adds a further twenty-four other types of women, who, he says, "are never to be enjoyed, however much a man may be tempted." Vatsyayana had listed only two.

In the end, it is only sex within marriage that the Ananga Ranga can truly countenance. Indeed, it is a sign of how far medieval India has moved that, in dividing women into four types according to their temperaments and physiques, the author makes each a symbol of salvation—of Moksha or release from further deaths and rebirths. "The name of the woman," he says, "is Nari which, being interpreted, means No 'Ari' or foe; and such is Moksha or absorption because all love it and it loves all mankind." The padmini or "lotus" lady

▲ *Royal lovers in Jodhpur enjoy the sophisticated bandhura or*
"curved knot" lovemaking position.

is accordingly "sword-release" or absorption into the essence of the Deity. The citrini or "picture" lady is "like those who having been incarnated as gods, perform manifold and wonderful works." She is "nearness to the Deity, being born in the Divine Presence." The sankhini or "conch-shell" lady resembles the Deity "in limbs and material body"—even as the man who takes the form of Vishnu bears upon his body the conch-shell, the discus, and other emblems of that god. The hastini or "elephant" lady is the "residence in the heaven of some special god." "She is what residence in Vishnu's heaven is to those of the fourth class who have attributes and properties, shape and form, hands and feet." In this treatment it is as if sex is a reenactment of different methods of salvation, a form of religion. What sex in marriage has lost in passion, it has gained in spiritual mystery.

A Woman's Sexual Needs

The same attitude illuminates the Koka Shastra. Kokkoka, it is true, does not use abstract terms or invest each type of woman with spiritual significance. The grand ideal of woman

▲ *The love of the courtesan Rupmati for the dashing Prince Baz Bahadur is celebrated in countless erotic paintings.*

has still to come. But he is acutely aware of what life is—of what is practical and what is not. He is concerned with how to make the most of sex, how to enjoy it, and how to keep a woman happy. Moreover, like the author of the Ananga Ranga, Kokkoka takes it for granted that almost by definition the partner in sex will be a wife. It is for the wife that he instructs his lovers in the four types of women, tells them how to induce orgasms and how success in sex is affected by varieties of organ, temperament, and disposition. Women, he knows, differ from place to place, and local customs vary. These are all matters which a husband must bear in mind when seducing his wife. For the rest, his account of embraces, kisses, love-marks, love-blows, love-cries, and sexual postures has only one aim—to improve the art of sex. But sex is nothing without delicacy and, as he describes physical details, he charges them with poetry. The Koka Shastra is not a piece of prose. It is very different from the Kama Sutra. It is neither brusque, stark, nor plain. Its descriptions keep nothing back, but Kokkoka's style invests them with charm and exhilaration. To read his book is not to undergo medical instruction. It is to gain a lively, new appreciation.

This revitalizing influence is carried further in Kokkoka's treatment of "passion love." The lover is admittedly the husband but the dwindling in romance, the loss of adventure is something to which Kokkoka's husbands have still to be reconciled. They are, in this respect, no different from those of Kalyan Mall. Like the Ananga Ranga, therefore, the Koka Shastra refers in part to ancient India. Although this "brave old world" had gone, some few traces of its customs remained and these Kokkoka carefully noted. He describes, for example, the kind of embraces possible during sudden slight encounters. "When a man meets a woman on some other errand and contrives in so doing to touch her body"—that is one kind. "If they walk together at a procession or in the dark and their bodies touch for a considerable time. This is the embrace by rubbing. If one presses the other against a wall, it becomes the embrace by pressing." Even in medieval India these casual encounters could sometimes happen.

Echoes of a Golden Age

In the Koka Shastra, Kokkoka models a number of passages on what Vatsyayana wrote in the Kama Sutra, injecting the drab present with an antique thrill. He describes things by which a woman may be "depraved." Vatsyayana had treated these at length but, in the broad context of ancient India, they were part of life. It was because women could be "depraved" by certain things that extramarital sex was feasible. In contrast, Kokkoka says: "Independence, living too long with parents, taking part in public festivals, over-free behavior in masculine company, living abroad, having too many men-crazy friends, the collapse of her own love affair, having an old husband, jealousy, and travel—these are the things by which a woman may be ruined." None of these were common in medieval India, but listing them inflamed the imagination.

The fascination in which the Kama Sutra was held is even clearer in the passage describing preparations for lovemaking. Kalyan Mall, in the Ananga Ranga, could not resist incorporating Vatsyayana's idyllic description. Likewise, Kokkoka felt unable to exclude it. He describes the "brightly lit room filled with flowers, the incense, the handsome clothes, the lively conversation, the delicate caresses"—all the arrangements of the "man-about-town" when he welcomed an experienced mistress. But the setting which in ancient India was a reality is now a romantic idealization. The lover—save in the case of the rich few—was as impossible as his mistress.

The same air of fantasy characterizes Kokkoka's last chapter on relations with strange women. Just as in the Bible the New Testament cannot entirely displace the Old but often refers back to it as the font of ancient wisdom, Kokkoka includes many ideas that are now redundant. He knows they no longer apply, but they were part of ancient practice. They can be viewed with nostalgia and excitement. He includes, therefore, the same time-honored idea that life and health are what really matter and that in certain circumstances "passion love" has to be satisfied "in order to save life."

Beyond Good and Evil

As a poet, Kokkoka's attitude to sexual passion recalls that of Shakespeare, which the critic Herbert Read explored:

His own involvement in the passionate varieties of love may be deduced from the Sonnets, which in themselves, all other poetry set aside, would for ever justify our human indulgence in this fatal emotion. I have no desire to be obscure in an issue where the critics of romantic literature have been so explicit. If I understand their moralism rightly, they would consider Shakespeare's Sonnets (not to mention Tristan and all the poetry and music evoked by that name) well lost if the institution of marriage could be preserved in its purity. I think that Shakespeare would have felt that life, in the biological sense, is independent, if not defiant, of moral codes; and though he would surely have held that life, in any sense worth the living, is promoted by a progressive refinement of ideals and aspirations, he

would have placed high, if not highest among the vitalizing and life enhancing forces, the poetic faculty. Whatever feeds its sacred flame is itself sacred and beyond our human conception of good and evil.

Such a view is strangely parallel to the Indian and some of the passages in the Koka Shastra—romantic, passionate, and intense—call to mind the vital life-enhancing role of poetry.

The Art of Sex

It is this same view, as the one described above, which explains how love and sex were treated in Indian painting. From the fourteenth to the nineteenth centuries—the period in which Indian miniature painting flourished—it was less the

In medieval India sexual games or fantasies involving swings were termed utkalita.

▲ *Perhaps the most human of all icons, this tender image of lovers embracing is a reminder that sexuality can bridge all differences of time and culture.*

act of sex that was illustrated in painting as the situations and problems of ideal lovers. Nevertheless, sexual positions, as discussed in the Koka Shastra, were sometimes illustrated, and these illustrations were often referred to as the "Koka Shastra." In the province of Orissa, in particular, sets of postures were engraved with a stylus on palm-leaf. These were not taken from books although they were often termed "Koka Shastras." More recently in Orissa, versions known as "brides'

books" were painted by the villagers themselves. All these books bore little relation to the Koka Shastra itself. Indeed, sometimes the positions were radically different, omitting some and adding others. Similar illustrated sets were produced in Rajasthan, in the Punjab Hills at Kangra and Guler— indeed throughout the subcontinent. When Lord Auckland visited Nahan in the state of Sirmur in the beginning of the nineteenth century, he found that the Raja had many such pictures with which he delighted the gentlemen as soon as the ladies had left the room. Sets of this sort were painted by courtiers. They were made for private enjoyment, for the intimacy of the bedroom, and were visual "aphrodisiacs."

It was also not uncommon for emperors, rajas, and nobles to be shown copulating. Such portraits did not demean the subject but testified to the man's virility. Sexual potency was deemed just as necessary to a ruler as skill in hunting or war. It showed he was a man. The full extent of these portraits has still to be discovered, but it is fairly safe to assume that just as Western artists—certainly most modern artists—have drawn lovers in union, almost every Indian prince was at some time portrayed accomplishing the "act of life."

Visual Aphrodisiacs

Pictures of this kind treated sex directly, and to that extent they paralleled the Koka Shastra. More often, however, erotic scenes were inserted in sets of pictures which otherwise illustrated quite different aspects of romance. When faced with the moment of climax, "the right true end of love," the painter was as unabated as the poet. The hero and heroine are reconciled, their joy is "endless," and they express their delight in passionate union.

Jayadeva's great poem on Radha and Krishna (see p.13), the Gita-Govinda, proves this point. As the drama comes to a close, Radha and Krishna make love. The poem was lavishly illustrated at Basohli in the Punjab Hills in 1730 and again at Kangra in about 1780. Both versions contain over 120 pictures. More than 100 of these depict various phases of the romance. Barely ten show Radha and Krishna actually making love. When they do, the positions they adopt are so conventional that there is unlikely to be a direct connection with any book. The Koka Shastra, despite the influence on it of the Kama Sutra, was based on the sexual positions contemporary Indians practiced. Indian poetry derived from this same source. When, therefore, Radha and Krishna are shown engaged in intercourse, it was as much on life as on the Koka Shastra that the artist drew.

Such pictures portrayed the sexual act with dignity and charm. The painters took sex and then with almost effortless ease enhanced the lovers' union with rhythmical poetry. Sex, however, was not their main concern. It was the lovers themselves—the changing aspects of their romance. In Rajasthan, Central India, and the Punjab Hills, artists constantly showed women in love—awaiting a lover, hurrying to a secret meeting, swooning at his absence. They were far removed from ordinary Indian women. In certain ways—delicacy, elegance, beauty, breeding—they might resemble the inmates of a ruler's palace. These were sometimes the pinnacle of aristocratic charm. It was their behavior—their absolute devotion to "passion love"—that bore no relation to actual palace life. Ladies at a Rajput ruler's court led as cramped and huddled an existence as peasant ladies did in twelfth-century France. It was only through prostitutes, singers, dancing-girls, and concubines that a Rajput prince or noble experienced "romance." In such circumstances, the ladies of Indian painting delighted Rajput courts for one essential reason. They were creatures of poetry, not of real life.

The Search for Romance

From the fourth to tenth centuries, the period when Sanskrit love-poetry was at its height, the lovers of ancient India were treated as models for lovers in poetry. Poets were expected to make their characters behave like these early lovers. Love could only be expressed in poetry if it was free, romantic, adventurous. Married love was admirable, but it was not poetic. Poetry involved the same attitude of daring abandonment as did extramarital sex. As a result, books were written in which morals were suspended and the lover was discussed as if he were the true and only subject of poetry. The first text to do this was the Rasamanjari of Bhanudatta, a Sanskrit poet of the fifteenth century. Women were divided into those who were another's and those who were anyone's. By "another's" was meant "married," but affairs with these women were considered just as valid a subject for poetry as any others. Poetry was the test, and Bhanudatta classified all types of lover and then showed using examples how passionate situations could best be expressed. His discussion was taken even further in the Rasikapriya of Keshav Das, a Hindi poet of the sixteenth century.

In both the Rasamanjari and the Rasikapriya, the actual mechanics or tactics of "passion love" were brushed aside. It was assumed, on the contrary, that no such basic problems even existed. The nayika (the mistress), if married, would always give her husband the slip. She would welcome her lover free from bothersome relatives. She would keep a secret meeting. It was unnecessary for poetry to say how she did this. The essential point was that she did.

It is to this tradition that the Koka Shastra properly belongs. Where it is not describing sex, it is hinting at love that has virtually no connection with life. Behind the Indian husband lurks the Indian lover, but it is in art and poetry rather than the Hindu family that he comes to life. To generate the greatest emotion—to excite, enchant, and soothe—poets and painters dealt with ideal love. And it was for this reason that the Koka Shastra included its ancient descriptions. Describing the exceptional as if it were normal gave the medieval lover the excitement he most required. It gratified repressed needs. It showed that romance was a continuing necessity, even though an over-strict society said otherwise. The less "passion love" there was, the more essential it became to believe in it.

▲ *Krishna, the "dark-colored one" and eighth incarnation of Vishnu, is the lover become god.*

Introduction *by Alex Comfort*

The Sanskrit textbooks on the art of love form a continuous sequence from remote antiquity to the sixteenth century A.D. or later, and on to the present time in vernacular versions and imitations. Most great cultures and many tribal societies have had a literature of this kind—our own Judaeo-Christian tradition is almost unique in lacking one—and have entrusted its production to poets. Persian, Chinese, and Arabic erotologies are nearly as extensive as Sanskrit, but the influence of the Indian love-textbooks in their culture is peculiar, because of the place which sexual imagery occupies in Hindu religious thought. For over 1,000 years these textbooks have influenced sexual behavior, art, and literature throughout Hindu India—and not only through literate people, for they have been embodied in "visual aids," such as sculpture, paintings, palm-leaf books, erotic designs, and posture-sheets, at all levels from the finest productions of religious art to peddlers' wares and bazaar ornaments.

The corresponding fear and rejection of sexuality, which is equally fundamental in our own religious tradition, has forced successive generations in Europe to turn to the Greek and Roman classics, or to the books that describe normal

sexual activities under cover of catalogs of diseases or of sins, to fulfill the same essential needs. Almost the first full-length picture of a different and less sexually anxious tradition was given to nineteenth-century Englishmen by Burton's translation of the *Arabian Nights*, and it is not surprising that they owe their first contact with Sanskrit erotology to the same translator, through his versions of the Kama Sutra and the Ananga Ranga. Neither of these, unfortunately, is up to the standard of Burton's Arabic studies, but they served at least to teach us the name of the great original source of Indian erotica, the Kama Sutra of Vatsyayana.

Origins of the Kama Sutra

The Kama Sutra is one of the world's great traditional prose books. Its author, like Homer and Hippocrates, is a name and no more—the text as we now have it quotes his opinions in the third person, along with those of Babhravya, Gonikaputra, and others—but throughout Indian erotic literature Vatsyayana is treated as the primary Master, much as medieval and medical literature revered Galen and Aristotle.

All the later erotic texts are verse renderings, subsequent condensations and expansions, or comments on the Kama Sutra, with the gradual introduction first of astrological and later of Tantric ideas.

The scientific attitude of the West tends to look to the most recent source; Indian scholarship, like medieval European, looks to the most ancient. In this case it is justified, for the Kama Sutra is vastly superior to its successors. Its real history is unknown—like most Vedic literature it purports to be a condensation by scholars of an older and lost work composed or commissioned by a God. It is said that Siva fell in love with his own female emanation Parvati, thereby discovering sexuality, and celebrated the pleasures of lovemaking in 10,000, or even 100,000 books. According to one version, these were reduced by his servant, the bull Nandin, to 1,000 books, but successively abbreviated by later sages. According

Erotic paintings, of varying quality, have always been available in Indian bazaars. Often the same images are copied and recopied by successive generations of craftsmen.

An extremely rare Tantric icon that is alive with potent sexual symbols.

to another myth, a man called Dattaka had the misfortune to pollute a rite of Siva and was turned into a woman. Later regaining his proper form, he found himself equally conversant with the sexual habits of both sexes, which, doing honor to Siva, he proceeded to set down in treatises. These traditions begin to resemble history at the point where Babhravya Pancala became editor-in-chief of a sexual encyclopedia. We are told that he entrusted the introduction to Carayana, the section upon coition to Suvarnanabha, that on the courting of virgins to Ghotakamukha, that on the duties of wives to Gonardiya, that on seduction to Gonikaputra, that on whores to Dattaka, and that on medicine to Kucumara. It was this encyclopedia that, says tradition, Vatsyayana called Mallanaga, as a religious duty in his middle age, abbreviated to become the Kama Sutra.

The Kama Sutra's Translators and Commentators

The scope of Vatsyayana's book is that of the hypothetical encyclopedia and falls into the same sections. The Kama Sutra has been carefully rendered in German and Latin by Richard Schmidt, and less well into English by others, chiefly in India. The Master of Love is a dry, realistic, and liberal-minded writer of plain good sense, with a Thurberesque eye for human conduct which is never quite satirical, but always close to satire simply by virtue of its frankness: "Rajas dare not do ill, for being like the sun, their movements are observed by all—if therefore they must be so rash as to undertake seduction, they should do it in their own palaces, not venture into other men's houses where they risk being killed incognito by some base person." The methods normally adopted by real, as against ideal, Rajas are then described. They may entice the lady to visit a friend in their harem—they may hire informers to convict her husband of treason and impound her as a hostage—and so on.

This pithy text is accompanied everywhere by a Dr. Watson, in the form of a thirteenth-century commentator of skull-splitting pedantry, Yasodhara, whose commentary is called Jayamangala. Most of the English renderings transfer large glosses from this commentary bodily into the text. Sometimes Yasodhara is useful—the story of Dattaka's change of sex, for instance, comes from his commentary, together with the more probable version that this Dattaka was the adoptive son of a Brahmin, who made up his mind to find out all there was to be known about whores, and became so well informed that the profession itself sent its finest exponent,

Virasena, to invite him to write them an official textbook. One authority says of Yasodhara, "he seems to be deficient in knowledge both of the Old Sanskrit in which Vatsyayana wrote, and of the subject he is trying to handle." He is informative, however, and seems to have realized that his master's work would one day be read by men unfamiliar with Hindu customary usage and mythology.

Indian Successors of the Kama Sutra

The date of the Kama Sutra is variously given from about 300 B.C. to 400 A.D.—there is little to go upon except the style and language. One would love to speculate that ancient Rome's own Master of Love, the poet Ovid, knew it—perhaps using it as a source for the Classical World's most famous erotic manual, his *Ars Amatoria* (*Art of Love*). The Indian successors of the Kama Sutra are of equally uncertain date.

Although the texts cannot be placed in any very reliable chronology, they fall into literary pedigrees by content —the Kandarpacudamani derives wholly from Vatsyayana: the Pancasayaka and Ananga Ranga form another unit, with the Ratirahasya not far off: the Smaradipika and the Ratimanjari form a third. Between the first and second of these groups, much astrology and Tantric magic has been introduced which was absent from Vatsyayana, while the third seems independent, describing different postures of intercourse (bandhas) and giving the rest different names.

▲ *The sacred bull Nandi, who guarded the door while Siva and Parvati invented sex.*

The late Sanskrit palm-leaf books produced chiefly around Puri, and now largely replaced by erotic playing cards, seem to represent a quite different tradition. One I have examined, probably of nineteenth-century origin, gives sixty bandhas that follow none of the classical texts, either in order or in character: most are complicated positions with the man in an odd half-kneeling attitude, and with much leg-crossing; they are drawn in "exploded" form and supported in the Persian manner by drum-shaped cushions. The sthita (standing) positions, the specialty of Indian erotology, number only three and are drawn without much practical conviction. In general I must say I have yet to see an Indian posture-book which exactly corresponds with literary erotology.

India's Sexual Renaissance

It is interesting to guess at what point the first revision and revival of the erotic masterwork is likely to have occurred, and what evoked the wave of poetic imitations of the classic original. At about the end of the tenth century, the city civilizations of eastern and central India underwent an explosive sexual renaissance. In the court society of rajas, such as the Kings of Candella, it gave rise to a wave of temple-building which represents the high point of Indian architecture to this day. Among its surviving religious monuments are the temples of Khajuraho, where ecstatic lovers have displaced the major gods from the places of honor in iconography, and the Sun Temple at Konarak. This vast stone replica of a wooden processional chariot is decked with innumerable figures of love-making maidens—are they heavenly apsarases, temple prostitutes (vesyakumari), or simply human celebrants of sexuality? Nobody seems to know which for certain.

The liturgical implications of the Khajuraho figures is plain enough—in the ecstasy of coition, man becomes god-like; while the Konarak friezes celebrate release-through-art and release-through-woman, the creation of elaborate sexual sensation as a positive work of art (they are certainly not there —as some modern Hindu interpreters suggest—to seduce or warn the sinner). The secular effects of this same wave of sexual energy appear in the nayakas and nayikas, heroes and heroines of the Indian romance-tradition. Their real existence was probably brief enough, but they have lived on as inexhaustibly as Theocritus's shepherds and shepherdesses and the knights of the chivalric period, in literature and convention, and serve as models for Indian lovers even today. Over this short period of time, the Indian tradition seems to have received a vast charge of psychological energy, on which its

▲ *A wooden carving from a processional cart of the kind echoed in stone at the temple of Konarak.*

art, literature, and religion have been running ever since—a charge which differed from that imparted by our Western renaissance, in that it lay wholly in the unconscious mind.

In part it seems to have represented the recovery by Hinduism of its self-confidence and *joie de vivre*, after the puritan pessimism of the Buddhist tradition and the diabolism of Tantrism whose adherents were perhaps the introducers of mystical erotism into Indian art and practice, but who mixed it with "such revolting practices as wearing skulls, drinking, howling, sacrificing human beings, eating food in skulls, and keeping alight sacrificial fires with the brains and lungs of men." India's sexual renaissance had more to do with love and pleasure and less with magic and ascetic practice—instead of esoteric and ferocious, it becomes joyous and popular.

The Western renaissance generated both emotional and intellectual discovery and eventually science. The Indian Renaissance, after exploding like a nova, seems to have been driven into the dark again—partly by the intensity of its own sexual emphasis. The gate of the preoedipal paradise banged

▲ *A page from an Arab law book, overpainted and sold as*
antique erotica to tourists.

once more—but the energy behind much Indian thinking had already been stored, and one has the impression that since that time almost the whole spiritual and emotional drive of the culture has been diverted to regaining the "oceanic" sensations of infancy by some other means. Hindu sexualism and antisexualism, the features of Indian art, the great erotic temples, Tantric sexual magic, and the erotic poems, all seem to be concrete manifestations of this original energy which comes to the surface again in the cult of the Loves of Krishna: at the same time, they continue a pre-existing tradition and are its logical sequel, a renewal not an innovation.

Vatsyayana's Readers

It is with the secular, not the religious, side of this sexual Golden Age that the erotic textbooks are concerned—their readers were men-about-town who decorated their pleasure-pavilions with the lay equivalents of the temple figures. Their contents predates Tantric sexual yoga, for there are no references to its chief doctrine, the "absorption" of energy from woman while avoiding ejaculation. The courtly background that he describes gives us some idea of the people for whom Vatsyayana wrote. The Kama Sutra says:

When a man has completed his education and acquired wealth by gifts, war-prizes, trade, or wages [i.e., the means suitable to each caste, Brahmin, Ksattriya, etc.], he should set up as a man of fashion. He will live in a city, a capital city, a district center or a country-town, or wherever there are men of quality, according to the needs of his occupation. Near to a source of water, he will build a house with two bedrooms and a place for the transaction of business, set in a garden. In the outer room, he will install a soft bed with pillows and white sheets, and beside it a couch. [one for sleeping, explains Yasodhara, the other for coition] In this room will be found salves and garlands left from the previous night, a bowl of cooked rice, and a case of perfume, citron-rind, and betel. At the bed-foot, a spittoon; hanging on a peg, a lute; a drawing board and ink-box, a book, wreaths of yellow amaranth; close by a carpet with a cushion for reclining; a dice-board and a chessboard. Outside the dwellinghouse, he will furnish cages of tame birds, and workshops for spinning and carpentry; in the orchard a well-upholstered swing, and a flower-strewn, suitably rounded bank. Such is the order of the house. "Rising each morning he will attend to the calls of nature, clean his teeth, slightly perfume himself, burn scented incense, and put on a garland, break his fast on a handful of cooked rice, examine his face in the glass, take pastilles and betel (or apply rouge and betel to color his cheeks and his teeth), and so to business. He will bathe daily,

anoint every other day, use sepia every third day, shave every four days, and depilate every five or ten. . . . He should eat twice daily, in the morning and the afternoon . . . after luncheon he will attend to such matters as teaching parrots and mynahs to talk, quail-fights, cockfights, ramfights, various esthetic games, receiving and ordering his storyteller, his pimp, and his buffoon, midday siesta, and in the afternoon, attend to his toilet, then to play—in the evening, music. After this he will wait for ladies who come to him on errands of love, and for friends, in his bedroom, which will be prepared and scented with incense. [If no ladies come] he will send a go-between, or go himself, to fetch them. . . . If the toilet of the ladies who visit him has suffered from rain and ill-weather, he will restore it with his own hand, or call on one of his friends to do so. This is the prescribed order for day and for night.

His religious and cultural duties follow. The rich Indian was certainly not—in his own estimate—idle. To be a nayaka one must be rich. Failing means, however, one can always lecture on the arts and so attain the position of chair-presser (pithamarda—professional conversationalist and storyteller, an Indian Peter Ustinov, if the comparison may be forgiven) and can by this means achieve the company of the hetairas, who are the first ladies of the land, in whose houses all cultural activities take place and all polite society meets.

This, then, is the nayaka for whom Vatsyayana wrote. He is a remarkably contemporary figure, lacking only an expense account and a heated swimming pool to make him modern. At the same time, the chief of his pleasures, for which all the others were a preparation, can fortunately still be enjoyed without cost, for more of us than ever before have privacy, plumbing, contraceptive facilities, and physical hygiene which no third century Indian gentleman could purchase regardless of wealth—we may regret that we lack his proficiency in making the most of them, but, according to Vatsyayana, we need only apply ourselves to learn.

A Sex Manual for Today

Some previous translators of Indian erotica, usually the least reputable, have made great play with the purity of their devotion to Sanskrit grammar and their innocence of any intention to provide sexual information for the unscholarly. This pretence seems hardly worth maintaining: for the overwhelming majority of readers, scholarly or otherwise, the chief interest of these works is in the information they give about sexual behavior in an unfamiliar culture, coupled possibly with a conscious or unconscious hope that the knowledge may give everything, definable by scholarship rather than trial—our sense of the oddity of the advice is very largely the result of living in a society that restricts our observation of sexual behavior. One can see just as many examples of nakhacchedya (erotic scratch-marks, the stock Indian love-token) on passengers in the New York subway as on any medieval Indian lady.

The English Version of the Ananga Ranga

There is an English version of the Ananga Ranga which has long served to introduce Eastern sexuality to English readers. The translators are F. F. Arbuthnot and Sir Richard Burton. If Burton—of the *Arabian Nights*—really had much to do with the actual translating—as against the publishing—of this rendering, his knowledge of Sanskrit, and, more surprisingly, in view of his other works, his knowledge of Indian erotic techniques, fall substantially short of his reputation for both. The text is full of blunders, and a good deal of it, particularly in the account of the bandhas, or postures, is a fabrication of the translators. I suspect they were unfortunate in the pandits they consulted. Some of the renderings of Sanskrit names raise the suspicion that this version was taken not from the Sanskrit original, but from an inferior vernacular paraphrase. This may explain some of these shortcomings: the style, however, is often unmistakably Burton's. Arbuthnot appears to have been the principal translator, and Burton probably "worked up" his version. The introduction contains one story that is vintage Burton and serves to introduce the poem I have chosen to render here—the Koka Shastra of Kokkoka:

A woman who was burning with love and could find none to satisfy her inordinate desires, threw off her clothes and swore she would wander the world naked until she met with her match. In this condition she entered the levee-hall of the Raja upon whom Koka Pandit was attending, looked insolently at the crowd of courtiers around her, and declared that there was not a man in the room. The king and his company were sore abashed, but the Sage, joining his hands, applied with due humility for royal permission to tame the shrew. He then led her home and worked so persuasively that well-nigh fainting from fatigue and from repeated orgasms she cried for quarter. Thereupon the virile Pandit inserted gold pins into her arms and legs, and, leading her before his Raja, made her confess her defeat and solemnly veil herself in his presence. The Raja was, as might be expected, anxious to learn how the victory had been won, and commanded Koka Pandit to tell his tale, and to add much useful knowledge on the subject of coition. In popular pictures the Sage

Standing lovemaking positions (sthita) are an important feature of Hindu erotic manuals.

them insight into their own. Neither of these aims requires any apology. At the same time there is so much of literary and psychological interest in Indian erotology that it is worth including some learned comment even for a general readership—those who only wish to get on with the technicalities of the sexual positions can omit this at their discretion.

Great stress has sometimes been laid on the unfamiliarity, oddity, and unpracticability of the content of Hindu sex manuals. Some of it is indeed unique to the Indian cast of mind, but leaving aside the mannerisms of the tradition—its mania for classification and its belief that there is a technique for appears sitting before and lecturing the Raja, who duly throned and shaded by the Chatri or royal canopy, with his harem fanning him and forming tail, lends an attentive ear to the words of wisdom.

The Author of the Work

Koka Pandit, it appears, is to be identified with Kokkoka, author of the Ratirahasya. From him, it is popularly known as the Koka Shastra, Koka's Book—the name, however, has become generic for the class of literature, and is sometimes applied equally to the Ananga Ranga. Burnell's catalog of manuscripts states, "This shameless book is a great favorite in South India, and there are several vernacular versions of it. The one in Tamil has been printed (in spite of the police). There were formerly in the Tanjore Palace a large number of pictures to illustrate this and similar books, but they have nearly all been destroyed." Luckily for the intelligibility of some of the bandhas (postures), they persist in Indian folk-art and can be purchased as palm-leaf books or as printed sheets for the instruction of rajas and plebeians alike.

The surreptitiously-printed Tamil version is no doubt the Kokkokam, attributed to Ativira Rama Pandian, king of Madura in the sixteenth century. This is a spirited production—unlike many of the classic treatises, which one can readily believe to have been written, as they claim, by disinterested ascetics. The Kokkokam is clearly the fruit of experience, and, if anything, better verse and sense than the original.

The Koka Shastra is well situated in its tradition to act as a specimen of its kind. Although it is in all respects inferior to the Kama Sutra, it more nearly represents the fashion in Hindu erotic science and the influences still at work in Indian sexual folklore. It covers both the early and the later traditions: that of Vatsyayana; the astrological system of physical types and lunar calendars for courtship (Candrakalas); and the influence of Tantrism—reflected in spells, japas (sound of magical power to be muttered on appropriate occasions), and far-fetched pseudo-medical recipes like that which requires "both wings of a bee that has alighted on a petal blown from a funeral wreath." In a sense the dilution of Vatsyayana's astute scholarship with nonsense is depressing, but in reality it represents a process that we see in the writings of many European alchemists. Like Aristotle, Vatsyayana had taken his subject as far as it could reasonably be taken by scholarship and intelligence without ad hoc investigation. The magicians "investigated" without the discipline of science, invented some results, and obtained others: they recognized the need for more empirical knowledge but had no reliable means of obtaining it. The later Indian erotic authors are wallowing in the gap between traditional scholarship and science. Of their works, the Kandarpacudamani repeats in verse what the Kama Sutra says in prose, with more or less additions and omissions, and the Ananga Ranga has already been translated. The other poems can most conveniently be dealt with as follows: I have translated a typical example of the whole series (The Koka Shastra), and added a number of glosses, in the traditional Indian manner, in the form of extended footnotes, and excerpts from the others texts—apart from the Ratimanjari, which is short enough to quote in full (this, so far as I know, is the first time it has been rendered in English).

The Koka Shastra

In view of the mixed character of its content, modern readers will be bound to ask how much of the practical advice given in Kokkoka's poem is to be taken seriously. The answer seems to be that much of it is uncommonly sound. There is not

▲ *A nayaka (the rich playboy of Indian romance) pleasures two ladies in his sumptuous love pavilion.*

Pillows are important accessories for those attempting the more athletic sexual postures such as sirsasana.

much risk of mistake: only believers in the Wisdom of the East who are quite beyond argument will try to follow the perambulations of the Love-God from the big toe upward according to the Moon's phases (though others who had not previously noticed it may come to recognize that in some women sexual response is cyclical in both time and site). On the other hand, a man who has married a very young wife could do worse than follow Kokkoka's recipe for handling her; most of the "outer" and "inner" embraces, adult people will usually have discovered for themselves—they may still be interested to see them so ably classified, however, for in our culture these common human experiences have only just come to be spoken of at all without embarrassment.

The Value of the Koka Shastra

The Indian erotic writings are based originally on astute observation. In this they resemble the post-Aristotelian biology and psychology of the Middle Ages, without its layer of theological dogma. They are not science in the modern sense —they have not grown from their compiler's own use of his eyes and ears, and they contain much evident nonsense. To

get a true idea of their merit, we need to compare them with the truly stupendous body of nonsense about sexual behavior which was being written in Europe by medical and medico-religious experts far into the Renaissance and on into the nineteenth century, and which has set the key for European medico-hygienic literature until the present day. The classic fount and monument of such nonsense is Sinibaldi's *Geneianthropeia*, which is the direct ancestor of a long succession of admonitory works, and the source of almost all the fallacies about sexual behavior that make up popular and medical folklore today. Even with Tantrism and astrology thrown in, the Koka Shastra contains materially less really foolish comment about human sexuality than many serious Western medical and religious books of, say, 1900. For these reasons we need have little scruple about leaving Kokkoka where the children might read him. If they would do better with a work of science, at least they will not be taught that sexual behavior is hostile, dangerous, and fraught with guilt, or that it will produce blindness, insanity, and pimples.

Kokkoka, indeed, unashamedly catalogs pleasures, where the Christian tradition has catalogued sins, threatening us, successively, as times have changed, with physical mischief, spiritual guilt, or emotional "immaturity" to rationalize its prohibitions.

The real value to us of Indian and other exotic works on sexual behavior is in the contrast of attitude that they provide with this tradition—they may help us to escape from it, even when they have their facts wrong. There are, indeed, Buddhist prescriptive lists of sins almost as hilarious as those of Sanchez, but no other culture has maintained its sexual anxiety at so high a level or for so long as Christendom. Kokkoka will certainly do us no harm, and people may easily learn something, if only an attitude of mind.

Bodily Types and Physical Proportions

The Indian emphasis on bodily types and physical proportion in sexual compatibility seems overdone to us—we usually assume in counselling that these are not factors that contribute much to frigidity, and attribute its commonness in our culture to upbringing. This psychological explanation is probably correct—at the same time, there has been so little serious research into the mechanics of sex that it is not really possible to contradict the Indian view.

We might be more inclined, however, to agree with the Plain Girl of the Su-nu-miao-lun:

The stylistic nature of the anatomy depicted in much Indian erotica
often provides inspirational rather than diagrammatic value.

The Plain Girl said "Men differ as much by nature in their genitals as in their face . . . some small men have large members, and some tall men have short: some lean and asthenic men have robust members, some big and robust men have small and flabby members . . . all that matters is that the organ should not be such as to hinder copulation."

The Emperor asked: "Wherein lies the difference between high-, middle- and low-placed vulvas?"

The Plain Girl replied: "The virtue of a vulva lies not in position but in use; all three, high, low, and middle, have desirable qualities provided only that you know how to make use of them. The woman with the middle-placed vulva is suitable for all four seasons and every kind of posture, for indeed the golden mean is always best. The woman with the high forward-set vulva is best on a cold winter night, for she should be taken under the painted bed-curtains and you lie on top of her. The woman with the low-set vulva is best in the hot days of summer, for you can take her from behind, while you sit on a stone bench in the bamboo shade, making her kneel before you. This is what is called making the most of your woman's anatomy."

One type of disproportion—in relative speed of reaching orgasm—is a much more frequent cause of maladjustment. There is not much ground for thinking that a choice of wife

▲ *Some texts list regional variations in sexual preference: ladies of Sind, for example, are said to like rear-entry positions.*

according to the Indian typologies, rather than by a direct experiment, would make for any better agreement here, though the careful preliminaries to intercourse emphasized by Kokkoka might. However, most counselors find that there is a proportion of unresponsive women for whose frigidity there is no obvious cause: possibly some of them are "mismatches" in Kokkoka's sense, and it is among these cases that a change of technique, or of lover, can produce remarkable results.

Sexual Positions

The proliferation of postures (bandhas) is characteristic not of Indian or of Oriental erotic literature, but of erotic literature generally: it represents a preoccupation of all sexually articulate cultures very like the elaboration of dance figures. The variety of these is such that they can be understood only with the aid of diagrams.

We would probably now interpret this human interest in coital posture psychoanalytically—and no doubt the emotion it arouses has unconscious origins—but at the same time there is a large body of human experience in favor of the practical advantages of such experiments. It is an amusing comment on our sexual performance as a culture that this should even need saying. "There are many males and some females," wrote Professor Kinsey, "who are psychologically stimulated by considering the possibilities of the positions which two human bodies can assume in coitus. From the time of the most ancient Sanskrit literature . . . there have been numerous attempts to calculate the mathematic possibilities of the combinations and re-combinations . . . Descriptions of a score, or of several score, or even of a couple of hundred positions have been seriously undertaken in various literatures. In view of the lack of evidence that any of these positions have any particular mechanical advantage in producing orgasm in either the female or the male, they must be significant primarily because they serve as psychological stimulants."

With the first half of this proposition, nobody would have any cause to quarrel. The mathematician Elliott Paul had a friend whose interest in permutation theory was so stimulated on this topic by a pornographic album that he became a mathematician (this is, in fact, a perfectly sober observation of one of the unconscious motivations behind the symbolism of numbers), while the more determined posture-collectors, such as the sexologist J. Weckerle, might well be reckoned compulsive. The latter part of Kinsey's remarks, however, is a little like the equally correct view that there are only two wines, red and white, and only two tunes, loud and soft.

Apart from the question of shades of sensation, clinical if not personal experience hardly supports the view that all postures are "equally effective mechanically" for a given couple, though this may well be so statistically for the public as a whole. Whether the Indian attempt to link these preferences with body build and configuration is correct or not, both modern and ancient counseling experience agrees that some women are emphatically more easily brought to orgasm in some positions than in others.

"It is recounted on this matter," says Al-Nafzawi, author of the famous sixteenth-century Arab sex manual *The Perfumed Garden*, "that a man had a wife of incomparable beauty, full of accomplishments and qualities, whom he was accustomed to enjoy in the ordinary manner to the exclusion of all other. This woman, however, never experienced any of the pleasures which should result from the exercise, and was invariably of extremely ill temper. The man complaining to an old woman, she told him, 'Proceed to the other manners of carnal copulation, and continue searching until you find one which contents her—from then on stick to that manner, and her devotion to you will be boundless.' The man, thus admonished, made proof amain of all the manners known to Science until, coming to that known as Dok el-Arz, he beheld his wife in transports of alarming intensity, experienced the most satisfactory internal motions therewith, and heard her say through lips bitten with ecstasy 'Now you have hit on the real way to make love!'"

How far preferences like these are due to anatomy and how far to psychosymbolism, is still an open question—the most likely answer is that, like our choice of sitting posture or of gait, they reflect both.

Sexual Choreography

The doubts expressed whether the bandhas, or coital postures, described in Indian books were ever really practiced, or are even anatomically feasible, are equally naive. Many, especially in the later textbooks, are certainly far more difficult than those in other erotic literatures, but this seems to be a direct result of the widespread use of hatha yoga gymnastics. The ability to sit, let alone lie, in padmasana, the stock coital posture for a padmini, or "lotus lady," takes Western lovers, unused to sitting on the floor, some months to acquire.

The coital postures favored in different cultures have their own character—partly dictated by customs in furniture: thus the Arabic literature specializes in semi-lateral positions and the Chinese in postures where penile and vaginal axes diverge.

A nineteenth-century illustration of one of the postures described by the Renaissance poet Pietro Aretino.

As to the multiplicity of postures that differ only slightly, it has to be remembered that they are intended to be used not only as single attitudes for a single act, but as sequences, like dance steps, with several changes during one union, in the course of which the woman should experience several orgasms to the man's one. Each figure must accordingly lead into the next and minor differences affect the sequence—like the difference between an impetus turn and a natural spin in the quickstep.

Sometimes this kind of sexual choreography has an even closer symbolic affinity with dancing—thus, by adopting successively the "fish," "tortoise," "wheel," and "sea-shell" position (matsya, kaurma, cakra, and sankhabandha respectively) one identifies oneself with the first four incarnations of Vishnu. Sceptics over such religious *doubles entendres* underrate the Indian love of living at more than one level. In the Indian tradition, indeed, this analogy with the dance is not merely arbitrary, for there are close affinities between the erotic texts and the Bharata Natya Shastra which actually deals with vaisika upacara, the practice of harlotry, as part of the technique of dance. Not only did the virtuosi of one art practice the other, but judging from many sculptural representations it was in the actual spirit of a dance that ritual, and possibly also secular, sex was undertaken. This presupposes a degree of control which some males in our culture find quite incredible, but which is common in societies that have elaborated sexual sensation. The secret of this is frequent exercise, plus a form of cultural

An unusual eighteenth-century painting of a Westerner enjoying the sexual favors of his Indian mistress.

desensitization: no Indian reader experienced much more anticipatory excitement from reading the Koka Shastra than we would obtain from a book on ballroom dancing.

Ejaculation Control

In India, and still more in China, ejaculation was sometimes avoided altogether, particularly by mystics and philosophers, from a medico-magical preoccupation with the need of the male to absorb the sexual virtue of the female without allowing her to rob him of his own, which is embodied in the semen. Sakyamuni, who achieved buddha-hood by practicing Tantric meditation in his harem, held that "Enlightenment resides in the sexual parts of Woman." Chinese sages in particular laid down detailed programs for the assimilation of this energizing principle from a succession of women, with the warning that what had been gathered with much labor would be squandered in a single ejaculate; if emission took place, the adept became subject again to the Wheel of Existence. The

superstition that semen is the quintessence of Man and that its loss means steady decline is still found in English books on personal hygiene, in defiance of the known vigor of stud animals.

Sexual Magic

The object of the Tantric rites which inspired the Khajuraho temples, and which are depicted in the sculptures, was to secure enlightenment and longevity—several of the Candella Kings who probably took part in these performances did in fact live to great ages. The Rajatarangini of Kalhana describes how King Harsa of Kashmir (c AD 1090) accepted a gift of slave-girls initiated into the Kaula sexual techniques and applied himself to enjoy them "because he wanted to live long." Gerocomy (the averting of age in man by commerce with young women) was a general belief in secular as well as religiomagical practice. Probably one factor in the popularity of complicated postures was the growth of a tradition of "picture positions," dictated by the sculptural need in Temple art to depict the lovers standing. Where the artists of Khajuraho require a lying-down position, for ritual or decorative reasons, to fill a square panel normally occupied by a God, they set it on end, supported by maidens, with either the man or woman head-downward.

Yoga and Sex

The influence of yoga is uniquely Indian, and also uniquely interesting in the discussion of symbolism versus physiology in the postures. Its widespread use as a gymnastic system (ghatastha yoga) accounts for the ability of Indians, modern as well as ancient, and of both sexes, to adopt unusual postures easily. One complete sequence of bandhas from Vatsyayana on, appears to derive directly from yogic exercises. This sequence becomes longer and more complicated in the later erotic treatises, until it includes really exorbitant *tours de force*, such as coition with the woman head-downward. The use of yogic postures in this manner would be denounced by some modern gurus, who hold that the function of hatha yoga is to achieve mastery over the passions to the point of "viewing all women alike and with indifference." It is defended by others, who point out that nowhere is it more desirable to master the passions than in coition.

One of the main objects of these postures is, precisely, to delay ejaculation. The reported "desensitization" of Tibetan Tantric adepts by erotic figures and exhibitions, if true, has probably the same aim. To us, it is probably more interesting to notice that the linking, in hatha yoga, of physically-induced sensations and fantasy-induced changes in the body image, is extremely similar to some of the phenomena which we see occurring in fetishism. For example, the cultivating of sensations of compression, tension, and fettering, and the desire to suppress limbs or to conceal external genital characters—as well as bizarre features such as inordinate tongue protrusion or the ability to pump water into the rectum and bladder. Not only do a great many of these fantasies turn up regularly in European sexual practice, but the tension-postures inflicted on the victims in imaginatively drawn, twentieth-century sado-masochistic comics have a strong tendency to conform to yogic asanas (acrobatic postures of symbolic significance).

There is neither time here nor, probably, enough fact available to go into the psychological motives of yogic mysticism. The overt emphasis in yoga on ecstatic experiences which look like a regression to infancy, and on the achievement of subjective bisexuality (the yogic adept not only learns to retract his genitalia until they disappear, but also fantasies a vulva in his perineum as the point of origin of the kundalini force which "ascends" to his brain) may mislead us into making too much of the symbolism. The fact that the fetishist gives them symbolic content, while the yoga-derived coital postures use the physical stimuli directly to arrive at enhanced sexual sensations, may mean no more than that such patterns are, to use Freud's term, "overdetermined," and the stimuli are effective in themselves. At the same time, in view of the amount of apparent aggression which we see expressed in Indian love-play, it is fascinating to speculate how far the multiplication of bandhas had value in getting rid of other pregenital compulsions.

The similarity between the use of yogic postures in Indian erotic science, and the use of contorted postures, erotic bondage, and the like in the sexual practice, art, and fantasy of so many other cultures, including our own, can hardly be the result of accident.*

Anal techniques—mentional in the classical Kama Sutra— are not discussed in the medieval Koka Shastra.

Stylized Aggression

The apparent violence of Sanskrit lovers, although in the written descriptions it appears to our culture excessive, is kept at the play-level by the rigid stylization imposed on it. We can easily overrate the part this element probably played in practice—the texts made it clear that the amounts of painfully violent behavior acceptable to most people in most regions of India were slight; they never emphasize pain-infliction for its own sake, and they enjoin complete conformity to the tastes of the woman as the weaker partner—none of these are aggressively sadistic traits: the biting, scratching, and slapping involved in the classified descriptions are probably well within

---

* In spite of a few bizarre features, quite the best European treatise on coital postures, and the only one to approach the Indian spirit, is that of Weckerle (L. van Weck Erlen (J. Weckerle M.D., pseud) 1907). He was a medical gymnast, whose motto was "Abgemattet ward durch geschlechtliches Exzesse nur der ungetumte Weichling" ("Only a weakling who neglects his gymnastic exercises is exhausted by sexual excess"). Weckerle recommended fitting up a "Sexuarium" complete with a gymnastic mat and bars. Any tendency to laugh is, or should be, counterbalanced by the fact that his book, unlike most erotica, is manifestly the product of personal practice and not, like the Koka Shastra, of tradition, or of fantasy. Gymnastic mats apart, a great deal of his advice is sound: his classification and choice of postures shows no direct Indian influence, and Indian works are not quoted—the convergence between Teutonic gymnastics, Indian yoga, and Chinese k'ung fu (medical exercises) as correlates of sexual sensation is all the more interesting. I have used Weckerle to unravel and identify coital postures mentioned in this translation.

▲ *A Nepalese painting from an area long associated with Tantric mysticism and sexual magic.*

the limits of sexual behavior by some normally adjusted people in our own culture. Comparative studies have suggested that the very boisterous type of coition in which these acts predominate is typical of societies in which there is a measure of sexual equality, and that the woman often initiates it. By contrast, there are no markedly compulsive features—the ritual flogging, for example, of flagellation literature in our own culture, never appears at all.

In the purusayitabandha, the position in which the woman takes on the male role, she consciously acts out the "domination" of the man. This generates embarrassment or is repudiated in many other cultures on grounds of religion, hygiene, or male dignity; it is fully accepted in Indian literature as a fair exchange. This practice is constantly praised in literature—it is Parvati's way with the Lord Siva, Lakshmi's way with the Lord Vishnu, and the way of the righteous. "There are men with merit, won in past existences, who sip the honey of their women's lips, while the women, on top, hair down and flower-eyes half closed, fall asleep from the languor of orgasm. . . . It is said that for a man with merit from past existences, the tongue is silent and the sound of her anklets is stilled, when the wife rides him in the purusayita mode." (Vasanta Vilasa.) According to the poets, she should wear all her most jingling ornaments (earrings, waist band, anklets). Radha rides so upon the Lord Krishna (Gita-Govinda 2–7), while "Lakshmi astride her Lord, lying supine, became bashful on seeing Brahma within his navel-lotus—therefore she shades His right eye (the sun) with her hand, to make the lotus close." (Subasita Ratnakara.) What is not unmanly in the gods is certainly not beneath the dignity of man.

The Woman's Status

Indeed, the real tenderness of man's approach to woman is a striking feature of the Indian, as against other Oriental erotic theories. While she is subject to the man, and to certain social penalties like those enjoined for her when he travels, she is expected to recoup herself in the sexual field. Vatsyayana's comments are all in this direction—in adultery. Man must consider dharma, though he may justify breaches of it if they are to his advantage: woman does not consider it, she loves regardless of it. As the obverse of this paternalism, it is the whole duty of man to please her sexually, restricting his own wishes and following her tastes and peculiarities even at the expense of his own.

It would be absurd to depict medieval Hindu culture as feminist in any contemporary sense, but its attitude seems markedly more congenial to us than that of other Eastern erotologies and can be much misjudged if we see it only through Victorian accounts of widow-burning. Most of the Arabic textbooks stand in a tradition that looks as if it has been heavily influenced by slavery as a domestic institution. They often cease to be erotic and become merely lascivious, the woman being less a partner than a subject for infliction, who should be amused in order to secure her cooperation, but who can be raped if there is no other way of dealing with her. Some Arabic writers give grotesque prescriptions for compelling a woman to make sexually effective movements, or even to experience orgasm, against her will.

A medieval Chinese household is depicted in the novel *Chin P'ing Mei* (*Metal Vase Plum Blossom*—a title ripe with sexual symbols), an unusually detailed fictional account of social and sexual behavior in a polygamous upper-class home. The mistresses and wives of the womanizing hero are expected to gratify him with no reference to their own tastes—to be seduced, manhandled, burned with incense, and otherwise subjected to erotic experiments—as well as being savagely beaten if they displease him. Though many of these sexual activities are traditional and are shown as being enjoyed, there is not much tenderness about it, and the women have no opportunity to express aggression themselves in sex—they do so socially, however, by intriguing against husbands and each other. The woman of Sanskrit literature is by contrast allowed, and in fact invited, to express it, to retaliate if the man is aggressive, to initiate aggression if she wishes. It may be a mistake to place too much importance on *Chin P'ing Mei*, which is a picaresque novel, and may bear no more resemblance to the real habits of the period than do our own paperbacks. The erotic techniques of the Ming and earlier textbooks are much less violent. Yet from the woman's point of view, this may not be a gain if it reduces the possibility of abreacting her frustrations in a conventional and accepted way that she knows will not threaten her husband's affection. The Indian woman of the Kama Sutra is like the secure child who is able to act out her aggressions in play without fear of losing parental love.

This attitude is typical of Indian literature generally. If the abandonment of Sita or the loss of Draupadi at dice seem incompatible with companionable relations or reverence for woman, we must remember that these stories are inherited from folk traditions. In their Classical setting, they owe their poignancy to the fact that later manners have introduced an element of tenderness into the story which makes the audience react to them, as we to Antigone's condemnation.[*]

The Objectives Of Sanskrit Literature

It is important to realize that love-literature in Sanskrit is not intended only to codify manners and act as a source of practical advice. It was also written as a guide to writers, painters, and dramatists, whom it provided with an *Affektenlehre*—a system of depicting love in a series of set classical contexts.

The two tasks, instruction in sense and instruction in art, were fully congruent. Both, in terms of the "threefold way"—duty, sensuality, and practical living—are functions of the satisfaction of the senses and the desires that go with them (Kama). Within this all the experiences, which we would call separately erotic and esthetic, are combined in a single type of pleasure, srngara ("affection" and "affect" rolled into one). This embraces the appreciation of beauty generally and the appreciation of the beauty of woman, the pleasure derived

from satisfying desire engendered by past experience of pleasant activities (hunting, music, or sexual intercourse), plus the "drive" that accompanies pleasant sensations, to secure their repetition or continuance. The "drive" is Kama—inferior, in the Indian view, both to artha ("gathering gear" or useful and profitable activity) and to dharma (knowledge of the right conduct, both religious and rational). Srngara is the emotion of those whose Kama is for the moment being satisfied. It is also, since "separation is a kind of love," the various bitter sweet experiences associated with the temporary baulking of Kama, by which its intensity is enhanced.

These are the subjects of art in general: love itself is an art, and art concerned with love has a double efficacy in interpreting or creating two sources of srngara at the same time. We meet the same idea in the religious use of sexual subjects—they are at once doctrinally instructive, leading us to one kind of release (moksa) through the truths they symbolize, another through the srngara of art, and yet another through the invitation to seek the srngara of sexual activity.

⬆ *Even the simple "yawning position" is learned only by practice, and demands considerable flexibility of the joints.*

▲ *A charmingly naive painting depicting a virtuoso performance of combined arts.*

Heroines in Indian Art

Apart from anything they may tell us about nayikas (heroines) in our own culture, then, the Indian erotic and rhetorical writers give us an essential key to the identity and iconography of the nayikas who are the favorite subjects of Indian art. Looking at this art without them is very like attempting to understand Renaissance painting without knowing the outlines of Greek mythology and the names of the more important saints. The rhetoricians laid down a series of situations proper to the depiction of love in all its phases, and nayikas and their partners appear in these situations for our recognition. Thus an Indian artist will depict the prositapatika (she whose husband is traveling) where a Renaissance artist would have entitled his picture "Penelope;" or vipralabdha (she who is jilted and left waiting at a rendezvous) where Augustus Egg would have called his picture, "He cometh not,

she said." The literary element in Renaissance or Victorian art, Christian pictures of saints, and Indian pictures of nayikas is thus very similar, and the artist in each case is assuming that we will know the background of his allusion.

In Indian art these nayikas are omnipresent. Those who dance, bathe, comb their hair, pick flowers, or make love in Rajasthani and similar paintings are often raginis—that is, nayikas whose conventional situation is matched to particular colors and musical modes. Others are specifically drawn for picture books of rasas—the rhetorical typologies or "flavors" of love and of mood. The topics vary from system to system, but beside the prositapatika and the vipralabdha mentioned already, we can usually recognize the svadhinapatika (who keeps her husband with her by her charms), the virahotkanthita (whose lover has been sent for but does not answer), the vasakasajja (who is waiting eagerly for him to come to an assignation), the kalahantarita (who has quarreled and now regrets it), the khandita (whose lover comes to her with a poor sexual appetite, bearing marks she did not make), and the abhisarika (who abandons all shame, braving the night and the weather, and goes to find him).★ Beside these we have the prosyatapatika (whose husband talks of a journey, while she, dishevelled, tries to persuade him to stay at home). We also meet a division of each category into "good," "medium," and "poor"—"good" who is angry only when she has cause, "medium" who sometimes picks needless quarrels but makes them up, and "poor" who scolds and finds fault with a blameless lover—and their respective men, the faithful, the tactfully unfaithful (daksina), the brazen, and the real cad. The source of these is in the Kavyalamkara and similar books, but brief accounts of them have been introduced into some of the works on erotics proper, such as the Ananga Ranga, in addition to the purely sexual typologies of "lotus ladies," "deer," and the like—categories based on physique.

Lovers in Temple Sculpture

In temple sculpture, and in particular the medieval temple sculpture of eastern and central India, nayikas are everywhere. Some are yaksis, guardian spirits, and female fauns in the retinue of the god Kubera—tall girls with snub noses, types of the "shell lady" (sankhini), who serve as onlookers, panel-fillers, caryatids, and proppers of doorposts (stambhapattalika).

★ "If a respectable woman goes on an errand of love, she keeps her ornaments quiet and hides her face—when a whore goes on a similar errand, she goes in conspicuous clothes, anklets jingling, smiling at the passers-by. . . . A field, a garden, a ruined temple, the go-between's own house, an inn, burning-ground, wood, or river bank are the eight places for assignations—or anywhere which is dark." (Sahityadarpana.)

Others are apsarases and surasundaris, types of the "picture" or "fancy" lady (citrini), heavenly assistants to the queen of all sacred prostitutes Urvasi, whose mission is to tempt and foil overweening sages when by austerities they have almost achieved perfection and are becoming dangerously holy. Others, with their partners, are gandharvas (angelic musicians) or kinnaras (bird-people) flying or dancing in tympana of doors or spandrels of arches and ceiling-corners. But many of them are straightforward human girls, with the typical figure and face of the region—thinking, playing with birds, titivating, combing out hair, and, above all, making love with their nayakas in the maithuna (loving couple) groups, which are one of the unique beauties of Hindu plastic art.

Only a few of the couples have succumbed to ecstasy, ignored the fact that this is a public place, and become lost to the world in petting or coition—most are coy or quietly amorous; figures out of any crowd at a festival who have forgotten each other long enough to be looking at the show. A few are married couples (dampati) who are there in their capacity as donors or patrons. Many are simply standing together, with a more vivid sense of quiet in each other's company than any other lovers in art. One can overhear their whispered conversation. Their confident tenderness often seems to have spread to other categories of being—the ganas, grotesques who are packed in at the bottoms of friezes and into medallions that will only hold a dwarf, or nagas (snake spirits) who with their naginis have silently intertwined the tips of their tails. The single figures, who are there, no doubt, in the character of apsarases, resting momentarily from their dancing, have become equally human; though alone, they do not intend to be so for long—meanwhile they are looking for thorns in their feet, writing letters, or gazing into mirrors—either blindly, in preoccupied appreciation of their own beauty, or more circumspectly, looking for the nailmarks left as tokens by their last lover.

The cumulative effect of all these women who celebrate tenderness and pleasure in the situations where our own religious art celebrates pain and deprivation—divine women who are not virgins, or will not be virgins a moment longer than they can help it, who take pride in the acceptance of love, not in its repudiation—is to give Hindu religious art a unique warmth in European eyes. Once we know its iconography and assent to its manners—to the many-armed deities whose retinue all these crowds of human and angelic beings form—we are likely to return to Christian religious art with an increasing sense of emotional starvation. Together with its nayikas,

classical Hinduism has produced ascetics even more grotesque than our own, but even this cannot make St. Ursula and her 10,000 virgins, or St. Lucy sending her eyes to her lover on a platter, anything but deeply distasteful by comparison.

When occasional Indians express the wish that the archaeological commission would "clean up" temple sculpture by tactfully removing the more erotic of the maithunas, as offensive to modern Indian prudery, one might wish to tell them that they are looking for obscenity in the wrong place. It would be more comprehensible, though no more justified, if these would-be iconoclasts sharpened their penknives on some of the more emotionally mischievous of our own saints.

East Meets West

The gain that modern readers in the West are likely to get from Indian erotic literature is precisely of this kind, whatever their motives in wanting to read it. Not many will learn sexual techniques that they do not know, or could not have invented for themselves. What is profitable to them—and us—in spite of the distance of time and culture which separates us from Sanskrit literature, is in the contrast of attitudes. It is liberating to find acceptance and pleasure where we have for generations been taught to look for danger and guilt.

▲ *A nayaka (hero) and nayika (heroine) concentrate on their equal and guiltless love tussle.*

The Later Erotic Texts

My method in giving a view of this long tradition is, as already explained, to translate the Koka Shastra, the oldest work after the Kama Sutra, and to fit the major divergences and developments of later works into parallel footnotes. Before going on to the annotated Koka Shastra, it is useful to survey the later and subsidiary works in greater detail. The Kama Sutra belongs to ancient Indian literature, the Koka Shastra to medieval, i.e., it already addresses a different kind of society, and incorporates ideas not known to Vatsyayana. The later texts run on through medieval and early modern times, spanning the Moslem and the Christian invasions and going on—in spite of the prohibitive activities of these religions and of "reformist" Hindus themselves—right up to the present day.

The course of Indian erotology after the Koka Shastra is chiefly imitative. Some texts hark back to the Kama Sutra directly—others add new material. Nearly all the main matter of later tradition is already present in the Koka Shastra, with two exceptions: the number of stylized endearments increases, massage, grasping, hairpulling, and finger games being added to kisses, nailmarks, and bites; and material is introduced from the rhetoricians, especially in describing the categories of nayika or heroine. Acceptance of oral sexual practices has increased steadily with the passage of time. (Some of these differences may well represent a shift in the region where literary activity was greatest—the late works seem to have their origins south and east of the early texts.)

After the Koka Shastra, the astrological classification of women (padmini, etc.) becomes paramount: it is the one quoted in India today. Palmistry, recipes, and spells become general; a few texts, such as the Ratisastra-ratnavali, bring in eugenics and the art of begetting children endowed with various qualities. These superstitions have retained their popularity and gradually ousted the more practical, and specifically sexual, instruction of Kokkoka, often, one suspects, as a consequence of the influence of prudery and censorship. This pseudo-eugenic material, absent from Vatsyayana, is actually very old, some of the instructions of the Ratisastra-ratnavali being taken from the section on procreation written in the Brhadaranyaka Upanishad.

The Pancasayaka of Jyotirisvara Kavisekhara

This treatise (The "Five Arrows," named after the weapons of Kamadeva, the Hindu Cupid), next in age after the Koka Shastra, belongs probably to the first half of the fourteenth century. It is written in elegant short-line verse, unlike the long lines of the Koka Shastra. The introduction is very similar to Kokkoka's however:

Perfume of Love, Comrade in intercourse with the beloved, Giver of
Joys, whose service is Desire, hail to the bearer of the Makara
(mythical beast of the Ganges) banner, the sole fount of blind desire,
Kama, whom living nature serves! Lord of the earth, honored for
granting us the means of daily slaking our devotion to him,
Worshipper of Srikantha on earth, treasure house of the sixty-four
Arts, pillar of instruction in music . . . worshipper of the lotus feet of
Parvati. To set forth the instruction of Kama, as given by the Lord
Siva, by Vatsyayana; with the additions of Goniputraka and
Muladeva; with a distillate of the wisdom of Babhravya; with the
teaching of the experts Nandisvara and Rantideva, and the science
of Ksemendra—is composed The Five Arrows, for the satisfaction of
all lovers.

▲ *A considerate husband gently stimulates his pregnant wife with an instrument admirably suited to the purpose.*

▲ *An eighteenth–century decorative panel*
celebrates the joys of lovemaking.

Hindu erotology stresses the esthetic importance of genital hygiene in both sexes.

The majority of the older erotic texts are dedicated to Siva, in contrast to the later erotic cults of Radha and Krishna associated with Vishnu. Some manuscripts give the name of the author as Jyotirisvara—of the other sources, Goniputraka is probably the Gonikaputra of the Kama Sutra, Ksemendra was the great Kashmiri poet and dramatist: Muladeva, according to Jain traditions, is the author of a treatise on thieving. From this introduction, the "Five Arrows," like Kokkoka's poem, sets out to combine the old systems of the Kama Sutra with the newer astrology.

First Arrow—the lover as city gentleman, the professional conversationalist (following the Kama Sutra); the classification of women, the astrological calendar of love.
Second Arrow—the physical classification of men and women, by body size; the geography of love—local customs; female genitalia; the philosophy of affection.
Third Arrow—recipes for perfumes and attractants.

Fourth Arrow—remedial and magical recipes, spells.
Fifth Arrow—female genitalia; sexual positions; love-cries.

This looks disorganized, compared with the same material in the Koka Shastra—the section on caresses and extras is missing, and two volumes of remedies and spells have gotten into the middle of the text. Other manuscripts which are longer apparently include all the typical caresses, as well as hair pulling and blows for the woman to strike in coitus. The Pancasayaka achieved nothing like Kokkoka's popularity with later generations; it lacks the Koka Shastra's verve.

The Kandarpacudamani of Virabhadradeva

This poem ("The Tiara of the Love-God") is a technically skillful and very faithful transliteration of the Kama Sutra (which is a prose work) into verse—an exercise comparable to the composition of the Scottish Metrical Psalter. It looks like the work of a court poet, who must have been a ghost commission by "god-like King Virabhadra" to carry out the transformation. The introduction is interesting in that it now genuflects to the cults of both Siva and Vishnu (see p.14)—

Glory in the highest to Bhairav [Siva]: as he looked in anger on Daksa, may he look in his compassion on his faithful believer, and may his Eye bring salvation! Obeisance too, ye wise, to Krishna, Master of the Arts of Love, who drank secret joys from the cherry lips of the gopis, sweeter than nectar! Obeisance to the Lord of Five Arrows, Minister of Spring-time, whose country is the lotus-eyed lady, and whose transport is the wind from Malaya! Hail to the clan of the Vaghela, honorable to Kings, and to the Enemy of Kansa [Krishna] compared with whom all earthly princes are of small account . . .

There follows a further panegyric of Krishna and Rama, and of their divine descendant Virabhadra, whose curiosity the work is commissioned to appease. The text is a word-for-word reproduction of the comparable passages in the Kama Sutra, diverging only to express, for example, King Virabhadra's dislike of the oral sexual practices which Vatsyayana describes (see p.83 note).

The Smaradipika

This poem—or rather these poems, for there appear to be more than one of the same name, "Light of Love"—are a far more interesting proposition, for they appear to represent a genuinely distinct flavor among schools of erotology, both from that of Vatsyayana, and from that of Kokkoka. It is interesting to speculate that the difference may have been regional—classical Indian erotics are supposed to have originated in the Pancala country in northern India, home of the heroes of the Mahabharata,[*] while the various Smaradipikas probably come from further south. The author is given as Kadra or Rudra or Garga. The introduction is very similar to Kokkoka's:

Hail to Love, who, though scorched to a cinder by the eye of Siva, yet made half his enemy's body to become feminine. Through the gentle god of scented flowers, the shame-fastness of the tenderest girl is healed. One Rudra, who overcame every obstacle and kindled love in this way: wrote the Smaradipika (Light of Love) to instruct the inexperienced and give satisfaction to the hearts of women, by collecting what was best in many treatises on the art. Those who have technique in love are beloved by women; those who lack instruction can only cover them like so many cattle. The joy of love-play, manifested in so many attractive forms, makes the human condition blessed, for not even a bull surrounded by a hundred cows experiences the joy we do. How to handle their own women, and attract other men's women, is the profit which students may draw from this book, likewise a knowledge of the different postures and actions. He who has lived one year with the Love-God's favor has lived for all time and counts all else as nothing.

We will first describe men, thereafter women; next the penis and thereafter the yoni, then the sites of love and the migrations proper to it; then the sixteen frontal postures with the six postures from behind, the two postures with the woman above, and the manner of oral coitus; the outer modes of lovemaking and its regional variations— the language of gestures, the use of go-betweens, the eight types of nayika (heroine) and spells, medicines, and how to get a male heir.

In fact, beside these matters, the text covers most of what is in the Koka Shastra. The chief differences are in the catalogs of postures, which have by now acquired different names, and the addition of the nayikas and the control of the child's sex at conception.

In the Smaradipika we encounter the material taken from the rhetoricians, namely the listing of nayikas (heroines). In the rhetorical works these are endlessly subdivided; the main and classical types, differing in name from source to source, but identical in essence, are these: "she who by coquetry and charm keeps her lover under her thumb (svadhinabhartrka);

she who, full of impatience, waits for her tardy lover (virahotkanthita); she who has sent for him and waits, looking out of the door (vasakasajja); she who has quarreled with him, and sits in a huff, repenting of it (kupita, kalahantarita); she who is jilted and left at a tryst (vipralabdha); she who drunken with wine or love loses all shame and goes to find her lover (abhisarika—iconographically the loveliest of the nayikas); she whose lover comes back in the morning tired and covered with marks she did not make (khandita). Her blend of fear and daring seems to appeal uniquely to the literary tradition: her abandon is the type of the Brahmins' wives who crept out

▲ *The Light of Love lists six different modes of rear-entry lovemaking.*

---

to seek the Lord Krishna, as well as of secular forbidden love); and she who sits unadorned and grieving while her lover is on a journey (prositapatika)." Alternatives, or additions, to the canon in some texts are "she whose husband meditates a journey, and who tries to dissuade him with tears and dishevellment" and "she who tosses on her bed full of unassuaged desire, while her husband practices austerities and ignores her love"—the goddess Parvati herself, consort of the Great Siva, figures sometimes in this role.

The Ananga Ranga of Kalyanamalla

The Ananga Ranga of Kalyanamalla is, after the Kama Sutra, and the Koka Shastra, the most influential of Indian erotic texts, both inside India, and outside, via the translations of Burton into English and Lamairesse into French. It was probably written in the sixteenth century, though its present form may be of a later date. The name translates as "The Stage of the Love-God." Its popularity in the Burton-Arbuthnot version is perhaps unfortunate, for, as we have already said, the pandits served Burton ill while the original itself is a poorer and more pedantic production than Kokkoka's. The introduction is oriented to the cults of Siva.

May you be purified by Parvati, who tinted her nails, once clear as the Ganges water, with lac after beholding the fire upon the Forehead of the Self-Sufficient; who painted her eyes with kohl after seeing the dark bruise upon the neck of the Self-Sufficient; whose body hairs stood on end with desire after seeing in a mirror the ashes smeared upon the body of the Self-Sufficient. Hail to Kama, playmate, wanton, dweller in all created hearts, giver of courage in battle, slayer of Sambhara the Asura and of the Rakshasas, who suffices unto Rati, and to the loves and pleasures of the world.
(The last phrase is Burton, and well worth keeping.)

The dedication is to Lad Khan, son of Ahmad Khan, of the Lodi house (A.D. 1450–1526), "by the great Princely Sage and Archpoet Kalyanamalla, versed in all the arts;" the present text appears to have been written later than this. The Burton version continues, "It is true that no joy in the world of mortals can compare with that derived from knowledge of the Creator. Second, however, and subordinate only to this, are the satisfaction and pleasure arising from the possession of a beautiful woman. Men, it is true, marry for the sake of undisturbed congress, as well as for love and comfort, and often they obtain handsome and attractive women. But they do not give them plenary contentment, nor do they

themselves thoroughly enjoy their charms. The reason of which is that they are purely ignorant of the Scripture of Cupid, the Kama Shastra; and despising the difference between the several kinds of women, they regard them only in an animal point of view. Such men must be looked on as foolish and unintelligent, and this book is composed with the object of preventing lives and loves being wasted in similar manner."

The scope of the Ananga Ranga covers the usual things, plus the Eight Nayikas, a longish section on palmistry, and (in Burton at least, though not in the Sanskrit texts I have seen) an extended account of the pompoir technique of grasping with the vagina (vadavaka).

She must ever strive to close and constrict the Yoni until it holds the Lingam, as with a finger opening and shutting at her pleasure, and finally acting as the hand of the Gopalagirl, who milks the cow. This can only be learned by long practice, and especially by throwing the will into the part affected. . . . Her husband will then value her above all women, nor would he exchange her for the most beautiful Pani (queen) in the Three Worlds. So lovely and pleasant to the man is she-who-constricts.

Further to all this we have a footnote: "Such an artist is called by the Arabs Kabbazah, literally 'a holder' and it is not surprising that the slave dealers pay large sums for her. All women have more or less the power, but they wholly neglect it. . . . " With this, needless to say, Burton anticipates the interest in kegel exercises today.

Of the astrological classes of women Burton says, or makes the Ananga Ranga say,

The same correspond with the four different phases of Moksha, or release from further transmigration. The first, padmini, is Sayyujyata, or absorption into the essence of the Deity. The second, citrini, is Samipyata, nearness to the Deity: the third, sankhini, is Sarupata, or resemblance to the Deity in limbs and material body, the last, hastini is Salokata, or residence in the Heavens of some especial god.

The Ratimanjari of Jayadeva

By contrast with the pomposity of the Ananga Ranga, the Ratimanjari of Jayadeva ("The Posy of Love") is a work of only 125 slokas. It has been published in Sanskrit and in parallel Hindi version, but not, it seems, in English. The content and the names of postures run parallel with the Smaradipika, some lines being held in common. The verse is elegant and compact—it is not by "the" Jayadeva, author of the

*A woman who has perfected vadavaka will
be valued "above all women."*

Gita-Govinda, but more probably by one Jayadeva the Encyclopedist; or by some other Jayadeva, nobody can now say. It looks a lateish work. The text runs:

In perpetual homage to the Lord Siva, Stealer of Hearts, the Ratimanjari is composed by the sage Jayadeva. Wherein is assembled by the said Jayadeva the pith of the ratisastras and the kamasastras.

Padmini (lotus woman), citrini (picture or "fancy" woman),[*] sankhini (chank-shell woman), and hastini (elephant woman)—such are the natures of women by birth.

Sasa (hare), mrga (gazelle), vrsa (bullock), and asva (stallion)—such are the natures of men by birth.

Eyes like a lotus, with little nostrils, round breasts a little apart, with fine hair, slender body:

Sweet-voiced, well-tempered, musical, beautifully clothed throughout—such is a padmini, and she smells of lotus.

An expert in love, not too tall, not too short, with a pretty nose like a til-flower, a jewel body, and lotus eyes,

With hard breasts that meet each other, a beauty; of pleasant nature and talented such is the citrini, and she is wayward.

A tall girl, with slant eyes, an admirable beauty, devoted to the pleasures of love, talented, and of good character,

Whose neck is adorned with three folds—such is sankhini, and a past mistress, they say, in love-play.

A girl with plump lips, plump buttocks, and plump queynt, plump-fingered and plump-breasted, kind, a greedy one for love,

Who is strong, loves violent coition—such is a karini (hastini) and she is hard to satisfy.

The lotus lady (padmini) is matched with the "hare," the picture-lady (citrini) loves the "deer."

The shell-lady (sankhini) is matched with the "ox," the elephantess (hastini) with the "stallion."

The padmini smells of the lotus, the citrini of fish,

The sankhini has a sharp smell; the hastini smells of elephant musk.

Young girl (bala), young woman (taruni), experienced woman (praudha), and old woman (vrddha) are the women one may take. And the properties of each when enjoyed are these:

Until sixteen years, a young girl (bala)—until thirty she is a young woman (taruni), until fifty-five an experienced woman (praudha), and an old woman (vrddha) thereafter.

The young girl is a lover of flowers and sweet things, the young woman is given to love-play,

The praudha to the give and take of love, the old woman to hard knocks.

The young girl gives a man pleasure and the breath of life (prana), the young woman draws out the breath of life—the praudha brings old age, the old woman brings death.

With the waxing moon in the first half of the month, the "trigger" of love lies in the toe, the foot, the lower back, the knees, the thighs,

The navel, the armpits and calves, the cheeks and throat, the scalp, the lower lip

The eyes, the ears, the space between the breasts, and the hair parting of the well-browed woman according to her kind:

The lunar progression of each woman resides in the hair parting, the eye, the lip, the neck, the armpits and the nipples, the navel, the waist, the queynt,

The round of the leg, the thighs, the knuckles, soles and surface of the foot, and the toes—migrating thus in the dark half of the month,

In the bright phase of the moon, love dwells in the left little toe,

In the darker, it is in the ventral side of the same finger.

In the bright phase of the moon, love resides in the right half of man and the left half of woman,

But the case is reversed in the darker phase.

If a woman is strong, she should be loved then in the inverse (purusayita) manner (i.e., astride on her partner, like a man): as the site of love changes, so should the mistress be enjoyed.

The expert kisses his mistress on the eye, the throat, the cheek, the heart, and on her two thighs—

On her face, calves, buttocks, brush, and the house of love, and on her two breasts: upon these the expert at all times kisses his mistress,

When she sucks in her breath ("makes the sound 'sit'") he embraces her with passion, kisses her cheeks and her throat repeatedly, and clasps her tightly,

Raising her pubis with his hands, himself crying "sit," and stooping to kiss her sweetly,

With a caress given to her breasts and his penis set to her queynt, the expert thus enjoys her.

With his nail-tips he makes three or five scratch-marks on her back, her lower belly, and her queynt and thus does an expert make love to a woman.

Having made such nailmarks and pressing her lips with his teeth he takes her strongly about the neck and strikes her queynt with his penis.

★ The terms are explained in the note on p.58.

▲ *First in the series of vibrant nineteenth-century drawings*
from the eastern state of Orissa that follows.

Having made her thus provision of a penis, he holds her tight, presses her two thighs together and without hesitation plies her [literally "beats her womb"].

Embracing the woman, stroking both breasts, her queynt, and her navel by turns, striking continually with his penis.

He seizes her by the hair with violence while battering her queynt, then setting a kiss on her mouth he strokes her queynt with his hand.

The padmini is brought to pleasure by stroking her breasts, pressing her lower lip strongly, and by coitus in the lotus position.

The citrini is brought to pleasure by the cry of "sit," by hard kisses on neck and hands, and by the hand on her breast.

The sankhini is brought to pleasure when man and woman mutually kiss queynt and penis and by passionate coition thereafter.

The hastini is brought to pleasure by seizing her forcibly by her tether-rope of hair, and plying her queynt with the hand.

Now the queynt of woman should be like the back of a tortoise, the shoulder of an elephant, lotus-scented, hairless, and well-spread: these five are accounted desirable.

One which is cold, deep, too high, or rough like a cow's tongue— these four are accounted undesirable by experts in kama-sastra.

The penis of man is described by experts as being of two kinds— the club, or the whistle: the first is stout, and the second is long and thin.

A man who is fond of women, a good singer, cheerful, having a penis six fingerbreadths long, and clever—such is a hare (sasaka).

One who is a paragon, virtuous, truthful, and courteous, having an eight-finger penis, and handsome—such is a gazelle (mrga).

One who is serviceable, uxorious, phlegmatic, with a ten-finger member, and prudent—such is a bullock (vrsa).

One who is tough, with a body of solid wood, insolent, of deceitful habits, fearless, with a twelve-finger penis, and no money— such is a stallion (asva; haya).

When a woman does not wish to make love with her husband or lover for lack of pleasure, he should make trial of the various bandhas.

Padmasana (the lotus seat), nagapada (the elephant foot), latavesta (the creeper cling), ardhasamputa (the half-casket), kulisa (the thunderbolt), sundara (the beautiful), and likewise kesara (the tress of hair), hillola (the wave), narasimha (Vishnu's man-lion) and viparita (the reversed), ksudgara (the petty?), dhenuka (the cow) and utkantha (the throat trick), simhasana (the lion seat), ratinaga (the pleasure snake), and vidhyadhara (the warlock), these are the sixteen modes of carnal copulation.

"*The sankhini is brought to pleasure when man and woman mutually kiss queynt and penis.*"

If with the woman in padmasana [i.e., with each foot laid on the opposite groin—the meditative posture of Hatha-yoga] he embraces her with his hands, and so swyves [penetrates] her deeply, it is the lotus position (padmasana).

If throwing her legs on his two shoulders, the adept gently sets his penis in her queynt, this is called the elephant foot (nagapada).

If he enwraps the woman with arms and legs and strikes gently on her queynt, it is the creeper cling (latavesta).

If he raises her feet somewhat up [skyward], sets his knees on the ground and forcibly massages her breasts, it is the half casket (ardhasamputa).

If he violently splays her feet apart and batters her queynt with his penis, it is the thunderbolt (kulisa).

If he raises her two feet, lays hold on her breasts, and drinks from her lips, it is the beautiful (ratisundara).

If pressing her calves and rubbing her breasts with his arms, he repeatedly strikes into her queynt, it is the tress of hair (kesara).

If he puts the woman's feet to his heart, holds her hands in his, and strikes into her queynt at pleasure, it is the wave (hillola).

If he presses her feet [together], violently penetrates her, and embraces her tightly with his hands it is known as the Man-lion (narasimha).

If he puts one of her feet to his thigh, and the other to his groin, this is called the reverse (viparita).

If he puts her feet up to [his?] sides, beats on the queynt with his penis, and strikes hard with his arms [?], it is the petty? (ksudgara).

If a drowsy lover embraces his wife when she is drowsy, thrusting his penis into her queynt, this is the cow position (dhenuka) [We seem to need "face down," but the text has "drowsy" (supta)].

If he puts the woman's feet to her throat with his hands, embraces her forcefully [or another reading, "handles her breasts"] and so takes her, it is known as the throat trick (utkantha).

If he puts her feet to his arms and calves, holds her by the breast, and so takes her, it is the lion seat (simhasana).

If the adept presses [encircles] his mistress with both his thighs, this is the love-snake (ratinaga), a device that steals the hearts of women.

If seizing her thighs, he strikes her with his hands and takes her with extreme violence, this is called the warlock (vidhyadhara).

One who brings a woman near him and then boldly seizes her two feet may be known thereby as a sexual athlete who has studied the sastras. All men should attend carefully to the study of these, acquire knowledge of love-skill, and make trial with women of the sixteen bandhas. Thus is completed the summary made by Jayadeva, the interpreter of sexual learning in the sastras.

The end of the Ratimanjari written by Jayadeva.

The Dinalapanika Sukasaptati

The Dinalapanika Sukasaptati, or Seventy Discourses of the Parrot, is a version of the popular Oriental story of the King admonished, and kept in the straight and narrow, by an erudite parrot. This is not an erotic textbook, but in the course of the moral tale, the parrot, the King, and others deliver lectures on all manner of topics, including sex. One is a legend about the origin of menstruation and the customs connected with it; another is a dissertation on prostitutes. The most extensive is a spirited list of coital postures, eighty-five by name and fifty-three in detail, which the King rehearses to himself on the way to an assignation (frustrated, unfortunately, by the moral parrot). This is an important source, which I have quoted a good deal, for the more acrobatic sexual techniques of late

Indian erotology. We can identify it, not with the other major traditions, but with the list in a so far untranslated erotic text, the Srngaradipika of Harihara (The Lamp of Affection). Harihara gives the names of the postures only, stopping short after the list, while the King's descriptions most regrettably lapse into unintelligibility and silence with only just over half the names accounted for (a pity, as the rest sound intriguing, and there is no other account of them available). The names of many of them are unique, as are the postures they describe, but if anything the tradition is closest to that of the various Smaradipikas rather than the Koka Shastra. According to Upadhyaya, the list recurs in the Saughandhi-kaparinaya, with an account of regional variation in the prevalence of the different postures. It would be interesting to know if this list

"A girl with plump lips, plump buttocks, and plump queynt . . . a greedy one for love."

▲ "If throwing her legs on his two shoulders, the adept gently sets his penis in her queynt, this is called the elephant foot."

supplies details of the last thirty or so, for which the king's, or the scribe's, memory failed him; the lapse is put down to the fact that the omitted positions are those "special to the woman," but we know some of them from other sources, and this hardly fits the facts.

When the twenty-third day dawned, the King went early to the house of the servant, meditating on the way as follows—"I will acquaint the servant's lovely-eyed wife with the arts of coition, eighty-four in number, and enjoy her at pleasure. Now the procedures concerned are as follows: if the lady, in the battle of the God incarnate in hearts, lies smiling, lotus-face upward, legs laid naturally, with half-closed eyes and the look of a shy gazelle, being

aroused to a moderate degree only, this is the position of love which all the world uses, and comes first in lovemaking. But if in privacy she rides upon the man, looking down on him, and making all manner of affectionate sounds, this is the reverse position. If so doing, she turns about, it is the turn position (bhramana). If, lying on him, she rotates wheel-fashion, turning to face away and then back, laying her hands on him [walking on her hands?] and kissing him all over, this is known to adepts as the wheel (cakra), etc. . . ."

Dinalapanika Sukasaptati is also alone among the texts in including a rhetorical classification of nayakas as well as nayikas. Male lovers are usually classed as devoted, courteously unfaithful ("Who still honors and loves his first wife, though he has others"), slippery ("who says hard things behind her back"), and the cad ("unruffled when he is in the wrong, unashamed even when he is struck, and lying even when he has been found out"); and ladies as good, medium ("sometimes angry without cause"), and bad ("always finding fault without cause, even when her lover is devoted"). Dinalapanika classes men as good, medium, and bad on another system. "He who bears a thousand insults because, singed with the fire of love, he loves a woman who does not love him, is the least worthy type of lover. He who is devotedly loved, but does not love his humble admirer, is a medium-value lover. He who loves a compliant lady and is loved boundlessly in return, o Prabhavati, is the best kind of lover."

As for the lady:

She who, though angry when she has cause, once her anger has flown away is devoted to her lover, skilled in the flavors of love, and in all activities—such is accounted the best. She who becomes angry without cause, is hard to smooth down, is sometimes bashful, sometimes not—such is accounted middling. She who is demanding, fickle, tactless in speech, and clumsy in action is reckoned as an ungrateful bargain.

Much more interesting is the fact that the author of the Discourses shifts the timing of the "monthly progression" of erogenous zones (see pp.62–5) from the lunar calendar to the woman's own physiological clock, so that it follows her own menstrual cycle, not an outside astrological influence. "The lunar influence touches every woman at the time of her purification, moving over limbs from site to site during the next half-month. The thighs, genitals, seat of pleasure, navel, right flank, and therewith the armpits, between the breasts, the nipples, the lower neck, the chin, lower lip, ear lobes,

▲ *The black-figured drawings of Orissa, here and on the next two
pages, have a unique vigor and intense erotic charge.*

forehead, the hair, and the fontanelle [on top of the head—through which the soul escapes at death], these are the lunar stations of love." One may reasonably be sceptical about the sequence, but at least it stands a better chance of being linked to hormonal influences than to the activities of the moon.

Other Texts

The Kamaprabodha of Vyasya Janardana, the Nagarasarvasva of Padmasri (said by some to be a woman and by others a Buddhist monk), and the Ratiratnapradipika of Maharaja Devaraja also contain lists of sexual techniques, and have been partly translated. They appear to be written no later than the seventeenth or eighteenth century. The Nagarasarvasva or Townsman's Compendium is a work of another kind from the treatises, more in the tradition of the Kuttanimata (The Bawd's Breviary) or the Dhurta-vitasamvada (The Cad and the Ponce)—dialogue pieces between members of the Indian demi-monde which recall the "Dialogues des Courtisane" of a later literature, although the Nagarasarvasva also has some

"If he enwraps the woman with arms and legs, and strikes her gently on her queynt, it is the creeper cling."

valuable comments on petting techniques, on sexual postures, and on the nomenclature of the stylized caresses. I have included these in their places as footnotes of the Koka Shastra.

The Nagarasarvasva is unique in combining kisses and sounds under a single heading, in a more elaborate account of tongue-kisses (maraichignage) than the other writers, in listing the holds (grahana) used to control a woman during intercourse, and in describing a magical routine of stimulating veins to produce offspring with different qualities. There is also a section on jewels and the detection of faults in them, which occurs nowhere else. This is the only erotic work we have that is Mahayana Buddhist in orientation—the invocation is to Manjusri and Tara instead of the Hindu patron deities.

The Ratiratnapradipika includes the most complete extant account of oral techniques, eight modes for man and woman. "Her mouth quickens now upon the shaft; when you stir to her lips and tongue-tip, she swallows it as deeply as she can and kisses when you cry out: This is Sangara, swallowed up."

There is a crop of little treatises called the Ratisastra of Nagarjuna Siddha, dealing not with erotics but with astrology, prenatal influences, and the like. They contain the kind of magico-sexual and genetical misinformation which was so popular in medieval Europe and is still influential in India today. Unlike the other treatises, this is clearly Brahmanical and pseudo-ancient, being in the form of a discourse given by the Lord Siva Himself to His consort. Some of the matter is ancient in fact, deriving from the ritual and sexual sections of the Brhadaranyaka Upanishad, but with an overlay of later astrology. Part of its popularity is that being devoted almost wholly to erroneous statements about prenatal influences and the like, and containing very little about sexual enjoyment, it has run into no trouble with the devout. It discusses such matters as the evil effects of sex by day, commending "the second and third parts of the night; the first and fourth are intended for the study of the sastras and religious books, and other knowledge-increasing literary works." It classifies women astrologically describing "the precious bed for the padmini, the beautiful bed for the citrini, the picturesque bed for the sankhini, the strong and durable bed for the hastini"—the last of these incorporating a provision locker!

Such then are the sources. Modern sexual attitudes in the West owe more to them, and to Sir Richard Burton, than most of us realize. The sex manuals and erotic literature of our own culture—with the advantages of science, biology, and psychology—are helping to bring the West to a civilized and guilt-free view of sexuality as pleasure and fulfillment.

"*The hastini is brought to pleasure by seizing her forcibly by her*
tether-rope of hair, and plying her queynt with the hand."

the illustrated
Koka Shastra

The Koka Shastra
(the Ratirahasya of Kokkoka)

▲ *Human lovemaking celebrates the union of Siva with Parvati. It is a symbol of unity and a sacrament.*

THE INVOCATION

To him who by his swiftness and his strength made even the Lord Siva, Victor of the Three Citadels, to become part-male, part-female, though he blasted him with a glance from his single Eye.*

Friend of the World, Storehouse of Joys, the fair, the divine, the God presiding over Joy in Existence; the Heart-born—to the God of Love, Praise!

When he rises in the heart as a conquering hero, the bees are his busy servants, the songbirds are his talented poets, the moon is his white umbrella, and the wind from Malaya his rutting elephant.

The slender woman is his bow, the jungle creeper his bow-string, and sidelong glances are his quiver. Hail to him!

This work was composed by one Kokkoka, poet, as a light to satisfy the curiosity of the Most Excellent Vainyadatta concerning the art of love. It is a concentrate made from the true milk of the most admirable Ancient Authorities, rendered down by zealous research to a sweet, precious, and youth-giving science, that which invites young girls to the enjoyment of love, and is honored, even among the gods, before all other studies: let the knowledgeable therefore profit by it and act upon it.

---

* Kama the love-God was commissioned by the other Gods to fire his arrow at Siva, who had retired from the world to meditate, and so recall him to earthly concerns. The arrow caused Siva to fall in love with his own emanation, Parvati, and thus to combine the Male Principle, immanence (purusa), with the Female, activity or manifestation (prakrti); this union is celebrated symbolically in sculpture in the maithuna groups (see p.15) of embracing lovers. Siva's first glance of anger blasted the body of Kama, so that he acquired the title of Ananga, the Bodiless God; the deficiency explains his habit of possessing human beings without warning when he wishes to become manifest.

The extra, cyclopic eye that Siva wears in his forehead, together with the Trivali, or three folds, about his neck, are the sole vestiges his murti or image retains of its original phallic character. Once in possession of a human body, Kama can be eclipsed only by a discharge from the eye of Siva.

The aim of such a book is to show how the woman who seems unattainable can be won, how when she is won she can be made to love, and how rightly to handle her in intimate matters. For where shall a man find joy—which is, after all, the sole substantial good in a world fugitive as water in a basket, and the capital fulfillment of all desire, equal to our thirst for the knowledge of Ultimate Truth—where shall a benighted man find such joy, other than by being thoroughly grounded in the principles, arts, and techniques proper to the God of Love? A man may be young and pleasing to women, but if he is not soundly based in the study of bodily types, of habits, of preferences, of local customs, of instincts, of situations, and of gestures, he invariably disgraces himself: of what use, indeed, is a coconut to a monkey?

In what follows, I have added, I own, to the teaching of Vatsyayana some matter which is not his. Now the repute and the credit of Vatsyayana are worldwide—yet where other authorities have made plain matters which he left obscure, it is profitable for the slow-witted if their comments are included, and such additions come fittingly under the title of "exposition." I will give in the first place, therefore, the system of Nandikesvara and Gonikaputra, then that of Vatsyayana after it.

A glowing celebration of sexuality by the modern artist Shri Om Prakash Sharma.

of THE PHYSICAL TYPES
and THEIR SEASONS

(The System of Nandikesvara and Gonikaputra)

▲ *The prowess of the god Krishna is celebrated in this image of him satisfying six women.*

There are four born types of women—first the padmini,[*] then the citrini, thereafter the sankhini, and finally the hastini.

The lotus-woman (padmini) is delicate like a lotus bud, her genital odor is of the lotus in flower, and her whole body divinely fragrant. She has eyes like a scared gazelle's, a little red in the corners, and choice breasts[†] that put to shame a pair of beautiful quince-fruits; she has a little nose like a til-flower. She is religious—paying honor to brahmins, the gods, and her elders; her body is as attractive as the lotus-leaf, and yellow like gold; her yoni like open lotuses. She has the soft, coquettish voice of a king-hamsa-bird. She is dainty, there are three creases in her waist,[‡] she prefers bright clothes, her neck and her nose are shapely. Such a woman is a padmini, and of the four types she is reckoned the best.

The picture-woman (citrini) moves well; she is not too tall nor too short, she has a slender body, prominent breasts and buttocks, the ankles of a crow, prominent lips, a genital odor like honey, and three charming creases about her neck. Her speech is staccato and her voice is like that of a red partridge. She is a skillful dancer and singer.

---

[*] padmini = "lotus woman," sankhini = "conch-shell woman," hastini = "elephant woman:" citrini is more difficult to render. The English word that conveys most of the meanings of citra (varied, multicolored, special, marvelous, whimsical) is "fancy"—"fancy woman" has, however, an unfortunate connotation. Another nuance of citra is "artistic," as of a picture.

[†] "Some say her breasts are the bosses on the forehead of Kama's elephant; some say they are two golden waterpots; some, that they are two lotus-buds floating on her pool. But I think that when the Love-God had conquered the Three Worlds, he put his two drums upside down!" (Srngaratilaka.)

[‡] trivali—the supreme Indian beauty-mark, and a sign of Siva. The folds recall the creases on the skin of the erect phallus—the god's sacred emblem.

Her yoni is round, plump, soft, quickly wet, and not overhairy. She has roving eyes—she loves the "outer" forms of lovemaking, is fond of sweet food, and elaborate devices [in coition].

The shell-woman (sankhini) may be slender or not so slender—she is long, long-fingered, and narrow-waisted. She prefers red clothes and red flowers and she is hot-tempered; she does not hold her head erect. The house of the Love-God is long, deep-set, very hairy, and her genital odor is acid. In intercourse she wets only when heavily nailmarked, for her love-secretion is scanty. She should be neither very short nor very tall, she is generally of a bilious disposition—her nature is lewd and treacherous, and she has the voice of a wild ass.

The elephant-woman (hastini) does not move daintily. She has stout feet with curling toes, a short plump neck and red-brown hair. She is apt to be spiteful, is rather corpulent, and her whole body, and more especially her yoni, have the odor of elephant-"tears." She

The posture illustrated here, with the woman's legs on the man's shoulders, is a variant of jrmbhitaka.

likes hot and astringent food, and eats it by second helpings, she has no modesty, her lips are big and pouting; in intercourse she is inordinately difficult to satisfy. Her yoni is downy on the outside and very wide within, and she speaks with a stutter.

The days of the lunar cycle upon which the padmini and the citrini desire intercourse are the second, fourth, fifth, sixth, twelfth, tenth, and eighth. For the karini (hastini) they are the ninth, fifteenth, fourteenth, and seventh; the remaining four (second, third, eleventh, and thirteenth) belong to the sankhini. The padmini should be taken in the padmasana position, the citrini in the "town-style" (nagaraka) [p.95],

the sankhini by the device known as reed-splitting (venuvidarita), and the hastini with her two feet on the man's shoulders. To obtain the best results, the citrini should be enjoyed in the first quarter of the night, the hastini in the second quarter, or by day. The sankhini does not become passionate until the third quarter of the night—the padmini is most attractive in the fourth and last.*

"Sweet-voiced, sweet-tempered . . . such is the padmini, and she smells of lotus."

---

* "The padmini never gets real satisfaction if enjoyed by night—by daylight she opens like a lotus when the sun falls on it, even in converse with a child." (Ananga Ranga.)

According to the Smgaradipika, the locale should also be adjusted to the lady—mountain scenery for the hastini, greenwood for the citrini and sankhini, flowerbeds for the padmini. (Smgaradipika.)

The later writer of a pocket-version, Jayadeva, is more chivalrous to the last two types and has different prescriptions for them—

"Eyes like a lotus, with little nostrils, round breasts a little apart, with fine hair, slender body,

Sweet-voiced, sweet-tempered, musical, always beautifully dressed—such is the padmini, and she smells of lotus.

An expert in love, not too tall, not too short, with a pretty nose like a til-flower, a jewel body, and lotus eyes.

With hard breasts that meet each other, a beauty; of pleasant nature and talented—such is the citrini, and she is wayward.

A tall girl with slant eyes, an admirable beauty, devoted to lovemaking, talented and of good character,

Whose neck is adorned with three folds—such is a sankhini; a past mistress, they say, in love-play.

A plump girl—plump lips, plump buttocks, plump yoni, plump-figured, and plump-breasted, kind, a greedy one for love,

Who is strong and loves violent coition—such is a karini (hastini) and she is hard to satisfy.

The padmini smells of lotus, the citrini of fish,

The sankhini smells sour (ksara), the hastini of wine (or, elephant-"tears"),

The padmini comes to pleasure by stroking the breasts, pressing hard her lower lip, and coition in padmasana,

The citrini comes to pleasure by the cry of "sit," hard kisses on neck and hands, and by handling her breasts,

The sankhini comes to pleasure when man and woman mutually kiss yoni and penis and by passionate coition thereafter,

The hastini comes to pleasure if one seizes her forcibly by her tether-rope of hair and rubs hard on her yoni with the hand." (Ratimanjari.)

In the Hindu theory of physical and psychological types (sattvas) padmini is the type of goddess, citrini of the apsaras, or divine nymph—sankhini of the yaksi (nature-spirit), and hastini of the raksasa or demon. The "wine" of which the hastini smells is almost certainly not wine, but the elephant-musk which runs down the face of a rutting elephant.

SPELLS FOR THE SUBDUING OF WOMEN

A nutmeg with the juice of plantain subdues the citrini; the two wings of a turtledove reduced to ash and mixed with honey, the hastini; Indian quince with sweet incense and tagari-root subdue the sankhini in a short while. When administered with betel, the following spells are muttered over the potion for the three types respectively:

Om! paca paca vihamgama vihamgama Kamadevaya svaha (mantra for the citrini)

Om! dhari dhari vasam kari vasam kari Kamadevaya svaha (mantra for the hastini)

Om! hara hara paca paca Kamadevaya svaha (mantra for the sankhini).*

"A tall girl with slant eyes . . . devoted to love-making . . . such is the sankhini."

★ The last two books of the Koka Shastra, which I have not translated here, contain pages more of this type of prescription—of little interest to even the most determined student of folk-medicine, however, for where the recipes are not straightforwardly magical, the ingredients cannot now be identified with certainty. The padmini is apparently immune to sorcery in Kokkoka's opinion—at least no spell is given here to subdue her.

of THE LUNAR CALENDAR

(C a n d r a k a l a)

▲ *Humor is a common feature in cart ornaments.*

► *A contemporary painting by Shri Om Prakash Sharma.*

In the light and in the dark halves of the month,* the God of Love adopts successive stations in the body of woman in a progression that begins from the left foot and travels first up, then down. So, in your lady of the Gazelle Eyes, he moves from the toe to the foot, the foot to ankle joints, the ankle to the knee, thence to yoni and pubis, the navel, the breastbone, the armpit, the neck, the cheek, the parts about the teeth, the eye, the face, and the head, and so back in reverse order.

For the head, then, lay hold on her hair; upon the eyes and the forehead, kiss her; press her mouth with the lips and teeth; upon the cheeks, kiss her in many ways; on armpits and neck, mark her with the nails; lay hold on her two breasts with the whole hand; between the breasts, strike her; on the navel, slap her lightly with the flat hand; play in her yoni with the finger, the "elephant-trunk game," and strike on her knees, shins, ankle joints, feet and toes with your own. By following the candrakala (lunar calendar) and varying the site of your caresses with it, you will see her light up in successive places like a figure cut in moonstone when the moon strikes on it.

The five arrows of the Love-God are supposed to bear the sounds "e" (for Vishnu) and "o" (for Brahma), and their targets are heart, breasts, eyes, head, and genitals. When these burning fiery arrows are shot from another's eyes and rain down thickly upon these places, then the love-juice of woman begins to flow.

Such is an abbreviation of the "calendar" theory as taught by Nandikesvara. The matter is stated by Gonikaputra more fully, thus—the resting-places of love are the

---

* This is the usual story. Dinalapanika Sukasaptati more reasonably starts the progression not from the new moon but from the end of a menstrual period.

△ " . . . polish the body of Lady Lotus-Eyes with the water that comes from the spring of her own love-juice."

head, breastbone, left and right hands, the two breasts, the two thighs, the navel, the genital region, forehead, belly, buttocks and back, then in the armpits, lower back, and arms.

Starting on the first day of the dark half of the month, the God begins at the lowest point and moves upward; leaving the head on the first day of the light half of the month he comes down again.

The experts of love denote sixteen daily stations in the body of your gazelle-eyed lady, like so many sparks of fire.

On the first day, the lover brings his girl to orgasm by embracing her neck, pressing kisses on her head, pressing both her lips with his tooth-tips, kissing her cheeks, ruffling up her hair, making gentle nailmarks on her back and sides, plucking softly at her buttocks with his nailtips, and softly making the sound "sit."

On the second day, she comes to orgasm if, lovesick from handling her breasts, you kiss the edges of her cheeks and her eyes, pull on her two breasts with your nailtips, suck her lips, tickle her armpits with your nails, and embrace her closely.

On the third, you will have her in season by holding her fast, ruffling the hair in her armpits, lightly nailprinting her sides, putting your arms around her neck and savoring her mouth and teeth, and giving the "click"* nailmarks in the region of the breasts.

On the fourth day, lovers reckon to hold a woman tighter still, pull the two breasts hard together, bite the lower lip, mark the left thigh with the nails, make the "click" several times in the armpits, and polish the body of Lady Lotus-Eyes with the water that comes from the spring of her own love-juice.

On the fifth day, hold her by the hair with the left hand, bite her two lips, and set her hairs on end with a sinuous nail stroke starting at the nipple—then passionately kiss both breasts.

★ Acchurita, a light touch given with all five nails (see also p.86).

On the sixth day, bite her lips—when she will begin to tremble all over; start with the "click" at the navel, then as if drunk with love, mark the rounds of both thighs with your nails.

On the seventh day, bring her gently into condition by rubbing the house of the Love-God with the hand, kissing inside her mouth, running the nails around neck, breasts, and cheeks, and so preparing the theater of the Deity for the performance.

On the eighth day, embrace her with an arm around the neck, nailmark her navel, bite her lips, make gooseflesh on the rounds of her breasts and kiss them; press her hard in so doing.

On the ninth day, let your hand play with the cup of her navel, bite her lips, pull on her breasts, set a finger in the Love-God's house, and mark her sides with your fingernails.

▼ *An exquisitely painted eighteenth-century ivory plaque.*

On the tenth day, you can wake love by kissing her brow, nailprinting her neck, and running your left hand around her buttocks, breasts, thighs, ears, and back.

On the eleventh day, she will come for nailmarks about the neck, tight holding, kisses within her mouth, a sucking kiss on the brow, a few blows over the heart given in jest, and a hand that plays with the lock of the Love-God's prison.

On the twelfth day, with an arm around her neck, kiss both cheeks and open her eyes with your fingers, give the sound "sit," and bite her within the mouth.

On the day of the Love-God (the thirteenth), she will come quickly to orgasm by kissing her cheeks, pulling upon her left breast, and slowly scratching her neck with the fingernails.

On the day of the Love-God's Enemy (Siva), kiss her eyes, play with your nails in her armpits, thrust your hand elephant-trunk-wise into the strongroom of the Love-God, and over her whole body.

At the New Moon and at the Full Moon, woman becomes passionate if you run your nails over the flat of her shoulders and handle her yoni and her nipples.

of THE PHYSICAL TYPES
by THEIR GENITAL CHARACTERS

(The system according to Vatsyayana)

According as their sexual organ is six, nine, or twelve finger-breadths in length and circumference, or in depth and diameter, men are divided into hares (sasa), bullocks (vrsa), stallions (asva), and women into gazelles (mrgi), mares (vadava), and elephants (hastini).

There are three "even" combinations in sexual intercourse—gazelle/hare, mare/bullock, and elephant/stallion. Gazelle/bullock and mare/stallion are termed "high" combinations (uccarata), mare/hare and elephant/bullock are "low" combinations (nicarata). The two extremes, "very high" and "very low," are gazelle/stallion and hare/elephant. There are accordingly nine categories of coital pair by size. Of these, the even combinations are considered the best; the high and low combinations are moderately satisfactory, the very high and very low are a misfortune. In the "low" combinations the woman never takes lightly and fails to get pleasure for lack of sufficient friction between penis and yoni. In the "high" forms, she is frigid and unsatisfied because continual pain and the tenderness of her yoni afflict her heart, and the heart is the essential seat of love.

DESIRE AND ITS SATISFACTION IN WOMAN

Animalcules generated in the blood set up in the private parts of women an irritation of desire which is little, middling, or great according to the size of the animalcules.

From allaying of this itch by the vigorous thrusting of the penis and the flowing of their love-juice, women experience the need for visrsti, which is the female counterpart of ejaculation. At the outset this sensation is unpleasant and brings them little satisfaction,

▶ A miniature from an unusual series, painted so that it can be viewed from two sides and intended for mutual enjoyment across a table.

This painting is said to come from Tanjore Palace, which once held a large number of images intended to illustrate books like Koka Shastra.

but at the climax they experience a discharge like that of the man, which renders them practically senseless with pleasure. One moment the woman screams, moans, throws herself about, and is distressed—the next she lies motionless and closes her eyes.

The speed of reaching orgasm in man and in woman may be quick, medium, or slow: there are therefore nine possible combinations on the basis of time. Both sexes can also be cold, moderately hot, or very hot by temperament, and it is important at the outset for the connoisseur of love to ascertain which—there are nine possible combinations on this basis, too. A woman who is strong as a man, who can take blows and scratches, and who actively desires intercourse is likely to be passionate; in a woman of cold temper the reverse is the case; and intermediate characteristics suggest an intermediate disposition.

An even match in all these three characters offers the best of coition—a mismatch in all three the worst of coition, no better than that of beasts. Other combinations give intermediate degrees of pleasure. The very high and very low combinations should be wholly avoided. With these rules I have put the whole matter in brief.

I will now describe the various types and their attributes according to the system of Vatsyayana.

THE PHYSICAL TYPES OF WOMAN

The gazelle (mrgi) has a shapely head, thick curling hair, a slender body with plump buttocks, little nostrils, flashing teeth, beautiful lashes, red lips, rosy hands and feet, delicate well-proportioned arms, oval ears, cheeks, and throat, hips and thighs not overgrown, neat ankles, the swaying gait of a mighty elephant. She is full of desire: her breasts are high. She is tender and easily moved as a stalk of bamboo; of moderately hot temper, greedy for lovemaking, eats little, has a love-juice that smells of flowers; her fingers are even, her speech slow and tender, her yoni is deep-set and six fingers in breadth and in depth. She is straight-grown and amorous.

The mare (vadava) holds her head half-bent. She has strong, smooth, supple hair, mobile as a lotus leaf; oval ears, neck, and face; prominent teeth, long lips, tight well-filled breasts, very charming plump arms, a slender body, and hands soft as lotuses. Her breastbone is broad; she has an attractive staccato speech, is restless with desire. Her navel is deep and quite round; she has fine hips, even, smooth thighs, powerful buttocks, a deep-waisted figure, a lazy, rocking gait, pink, well-proportioned feet, and a fickle heart. She loves sleep and eating; she is affectionate. Her love-juice, which

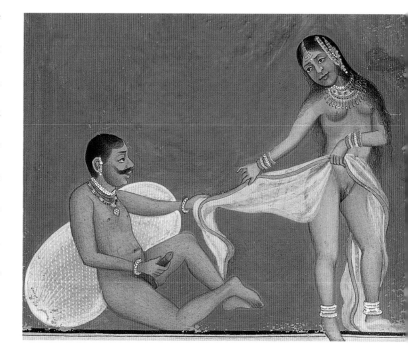

Commissioned early this century, the Uttar Pradesh series is a unique collection of erotic portraits of clearly identifiable individuals.

flows readily in intercourse from start to finish, has a pleasant odor like sesame meal and is yellow. She is fit at any moment for the love-struggle, and has a nine-finger yoni.

The elephant (hastini) has a broad brow, broad cheeks, ears, and nostrils, short plump fingers, feet, arms, and thighs, a short, strong, and slightly bent neck, teeth which show, and strong black hair. She is perpetually sick for lovemaking; her voice is in her throat and deep as an elephant's; her body is strong; she has a broad pendant belly and lips. Her love-juice is abundant; she is red-eyed, quarrelsome, with a genital odor like the "tears" of a rutting elephant. She commonly has many secret vices, is unusually full of faults, can be won by brute force, and has a twelve-finger yoni, which is the number ascribed to the Sun.

THE PHYSICAL TYPES OF MAN

The hare (sasa) has big, red eyes, small even teeth, a round face; he dresses well, has well-shaped, soft, pink hands with narrow fingers, is well-spoken, volatile in mood, soft-haired. His neck is not too long; he is lean about the knees, thighs, hands, genitals, and feet. His appetite is small, his manner unassuming, and he is not much given to copulation. He shines with cleanliness; he makes money easily, success inflates him; his seminal fluid has a pleasant odor—he is attractive to women and affectionate.

The bullock (vrsa) has a strong, erect head, a very broad face and brow, a stout neck, fleshy ears, a rounded tortoise-shaped body; he is stout, with deep armpits, long dangling arms, red hands and lips. His eyes are like a lotus-leaf, red in the corners, which have fine long lashes and stare straight at you. He is spirited, with a swinging free gait, soft-spoken, tough, generous, inclined to sleep long, broadminded, tall but gangling, passionate in coition, capable of repeated orgasm, phlegmatic, well-preserved in middle age, inclined to be over-corpulent, happy with any woman, and having a penis nine fingers long or less.

Stallion (asva) is the name given to him who has a very long, but not lean, face, ears, neck, lips and feet, fatty armpits, fleshy arms and strong, soft, thick hair. He is violently jealous; he has arched feet, bowed knees, good fingernails, long fingers, large mobile eyes; he is powerfully built but lazy. His voice is deep and pleasant; he walks fast; his thighs are plump. He is fond of women, talks loudly, is overendowed with both bony and seminal matter, and tormented by lust. His semen is salt, yellow like fresh butter, and very abundant. He has a twelve-finger penis and a bulging breastbone of the same length.

We may also encounter individuals, where the size of the sexual organs diverges from these standards. These represent very extreme or very poor examples of their type. Mixed types are also encountered, with intermediate attributes. In dealing with these, the expert will go by the sum total of characters present.

▲ Commissioned early this century, the Uttar Pradesh series is a unique collection of erotic portraits.

of WOMEN *by* THEIR AGES,
TEMPERAMENTS, *and* DISPOSITIONS

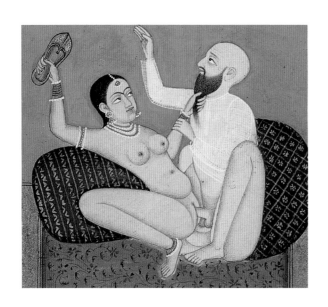

⌄ *This aged lover should have paid more attention to the Hindu erotic manuals.*

► *A courtesan displays the jewelry that is both the reward for her lovemaking and a means of enhancing her virtuoso skills in the art.*

OF AGES

Until her sixteenth year, a girl is called bala. From sixteen to thirty, she is taruni (a young woman), from thirty to fifty, she is praudha (experienced)—from then on, she is vrddha (old).[*]

(A woman who has long been away from her husband is thin, dark, fragile, and lethargic, with deep armpits. A woman who is enjoying regular intercourse is strong, golden-skinned, and shining, with shallow armpits. Admixtures of these characters give an intermediate type.)

Now these are the characteristics of each:

A young girl who is not yet mature must be approached by way of the "outer" forms of love-making—a grown woman who is fully relaxed sets her heart on the "inner" forms.

The girl (bala) can be won by giving her betel-fruit, promising her elaborate meals, by recounting all manner of wonders to her, by the arts, and by games. The young woman (taruni) responds to presents of alluring jewelry. The grown woman (praudha) loves nothing more than long-lasting love-play. The old woman is won by courteous speeches and by stuffing her with promises of marriage.

[*] Sexual contact with each age has its effects on the man: "Sleep with the bala and get the breath of life; sleep with the taruni and spend the breath of life; sleep with the praudha and hasten old age; sleep with the vrddha and hasten death." (Ratimanjari.)

OF TEMPERAMENTS

The phlegmatic woman has knees, joints, and knuckles that are not prominent; gentle, quiet speech; and is soft as a lotus. A woman with hot limbs and prominent joints is of the bilious temperament. The woman of aerial temperament is barren— her limbs are part-cold, part-hot. The phlegmatic woman is hot, but the bilious has a body as cool as new butter—she is also proud.

The rules for intercourse with these three types (aerial, bilious, phlegmatic) are these: in passion and speed of orgasm, they are respectively slow, medium, and fast; moist, hot, and deep-sexed; and most ready for coition in the cold of winter, in the rainy season, and in the month Madhu.

"A woman who is enjoying regular intercourse is strong, golden-skinned and shining. . . . "

The diagnostic signs of these types to be observed in practice are given by the Gunapataka* more fully as follows:

---

* A famous medical treatise, now apparently lost.

The phlegmatic woman has fine nails, eyes, and teeth; is easy-tempered, faithful, proud, and has a cool, plump yoni that is agreeable to the touch.

The bilious woman is by nature flighty, and is intermediate in characters between the other two types. She is light-skinned, with hard breasts and rosy nails and eyes; her sweat is strong-smelling; she is alternately angry and devoted; she loves cool and hates hot weather; she is hot herself; she has a soft yoni; she is wily, competent, and always most tender in intercourse.

The aerial woman is worth least of the three: she is coarse, gadabout, and extremely talkative. Her hair is the color of slightly singed wood; she eats a great deal, has a cool body, and hard hairs with definite points to them; she is strong, her nails and eyes are dark-colored, and her yoni is of the texture of a cow's tongue, rough to the touch.

Intermediates between these types can be recognized by a combination of characters.

A wooden carving of a female nature spirit, embodying animal and elemental forces.

OF THE SATTVAS *(dispositions)*

The goddess type (devasattva) has a clean, fragrant body, and a serene face. She is rich in money and servants, and very beautiful.

The human type (narasattva) is of even disposition, versatile, loves entertaining and company, and can fast without losing strength.

The snake-spirit type (nagasattva) sighs and yawns a great deal, loves to trail about, is always falling asleep, and suddenly becoming active again.

The nature-spirit type (yaksasattva) has absolutely no respect for dignified persons, likes public gardens and taverns, delights in coition, and is liable to tantrums.

The gandharva (angel) type (gandharvasattva) is the title given to a woman with no angry emotions, who wears divine and dazzling clothes, loves garlands, perfumes and incense, is a trained singer and player, and is educated in the sixty-four Arts.

The devil type (pisacasattva) is puffed up with pride, eats far too much, has a body that is hot to the touch, and loves red meat and strong drink.

The artist's style clearly shows Western influence, but its guiltless portrayal of sexuality is quintessentially Hindu.

The crow type (kakasattva) lets her eyes roll in all directions, overeats until she is sick, and is full of unprofitable activity.

A woman with a wandering eye, who loves to use nails and teeth in the love-battle, and is of a fickle disposition, is said to be monkey-minded (vanaraprakrti); while one who gives saucy and rude answers, and loves to run loose with men, is the donkey type (kharasattvika).*

SUMMARY CONCERNING THE TYPES OF WOMAN

Of these various typologies—by size of organs, by age, by constitution, by disposition—that by constitution is sovereign. Karnisuta and other authors have laid down the manner of lovemaking proper to each. This summary of the matter should be noted:

---

* This Thurberesque list by no means exhausts the sattvas; as with the rasas, raginis, and other typologies, the rhetoricians delighted in multiplying them indefinitely. The rather pedantic Bharatiyanatyasastra text gives twenty-two sattvas, dispositions that are supposed to reflect the residues of a past, animal or other, incarnation—applied to acquaintances, they make an admirable party game.

A pretty girl, of the phlegmatic constitution; a mare- or gazelle-woman; an angel, yaksi, human, or goddess-type; a young girl or one in the freshness of youth—this is the ideal for those who desire pleasure in this world.

OF THINGS BY WHICH A WOMAN MAY BE DEPRAVED

(*strinasahetu*)

Independence, living too long with parents, taking part in public festivals, over-free behavior in masculine company, living abroad, having too many man-crazy friends, the collapse of her own love affair, having an old husband, jealousy, and travel—these are the things by which a woman may be ruined.

OF AVERSION TO MEN AND ITS CAUSES (*Vairagyahetu*)

Cowardice, lack of stamina, uncleanliness, avarice, ignorance of the right times for lovemaking, grossness, excessive cruelty in lovemaking, refusal to give them ornaments, unjust railing at faults, oppressive sexual tastes, neglect, and meanness inspire in women the greatest aversion. A woman will neither take note of such a man nor honor his friends and acquaintances. She will resist him, become weary in his company, and be pleased to part from him. If he kisses her, she will turn her face away; she will have no wish to receive favors from him, be jealous, refuse to answer when he speaks, resent it when he touches her, and feign sleep when he comes to bed. These are the signs of aversion.

OF DESIRE

The signs of desire, according to the Gunapataka, are identical both in women who have already tasted coition and in those who have not.

A girl in love sucks at her lips, her eyes stray about like fish in a river pool, she wears flowers in her hair, binds it up, and then lets it down again. Her breasts show through her

A vivid painting on paper in the lively Orissan style.

clothes, her buttocks likewise, and her girdle keeps slipping, however tightly she ties it.* All these things serve in a woman to make known that she is in love. If she longs for a man as often as his face, his good looks, his conversation, his virtues, and his affection are praised; and if, when he is not present, she delights in hearing news of his acquaintances and his friends—this, too, is a sign that she is in love.

THE BEST TIMES FOR INTERCOURSE

Desire for coition is strong in women when they are tired from travel, convalescent from a fever, weary with dancing, about a month after delivery, and in the sixth month of pregnancy. The most pleasing occasions for intercourse are said to be at reunion after a long parting, reconciliation after a quarrel, the first intercourse after menstrual purification, and when the lady has been drinking.

At the first love-battle† women commonly show only moderate passion and take a long time to reach orgasm—at the second they are more passionate and come more quickly. In men, the reverse is true

---

* No garment is more fully an extension of its wearer, state of mind and all, than the sari. It can be like sheet metal—or it can simply dissolve. "When he came to my bed," writes the poetess Vikatanitamba, "the knot of my dress untied itself and fell to my hips, checked by my girdle until that too dissolved. So far I clearly remember— but when he put his hand to me, o friend, may I die if I remember any more—of myself, of him, of what he did to me!"

† The first of a series of unions: not loss of virginity.

OF THE ORGASM, AND ITS RESTRAINT

Men normally attain orgasm more quickly than women. Knowing this, the man must handle the woman in such a way that she is thoroughly moist before intercourse takes place.

By knowing the influence of regional preferences, of seasons, and of type, and by regulating the use of "outer" embraces accordingly, he can make sure that, being thoroughly aroused and deeply in love, she will wet quickly and be quickly satisfied.

"Love that arises from likemindedness between lovers . . . is accounted the deepest of all."

However passionate he may be, a man can remain indefinitely potent if during intercourse he directs his thoughts to rivers, woods, caves, mountains, or other pleasant places, and proceeds gently and slowly. If he imagines a nimble monkey swinging on the branch of a tree, he will not ejaculate even though his semen is already at the tip of his penis.

OF THE FORMS OF PRITI *(desire)*

A love that arises from an activity, such as hunting, dancing, vina-playing, or painting is called by the learned conditioned love (abhyasiki priti). That which comes neither from an activity nor from circumstances, but arises spontaneously in the heart, like the desire of eunuchs for oral intercourse, or of men and women for kissing and embracing, is called spontaneous (abhimanaja). Love that arises from likemindedness between lovers is called spiritual (vaisayiki): it arises from the soul and is accounted the deepest of all.

What we have so far said of personal differences—of bodily type, of age, and of other matters—and what we shall next say of local usages and tastes, all this should be born in mind by the lover when he approaches a girl.

of WOMEN *by* CUSTOM *and* PLACE

(D e s a s a t m y a m)

► A painting from a series commissioned by Uttar Pradesh around 1900.

The women of the Central Provinces have five manners, and dislike nail- and tooth-marking and kisses; the women of Avanti and Balh also: they like the more advanced kinds of coition.*

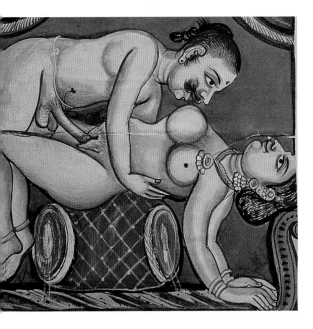

▲ "The women of Dravidia . . . have a very abundant love-juice."

The woman of Abhira likes embraces, but not nail- and toothmarks; she enjoys erotic blows and her heart can be won by kisses. The Malava woman has similar tastes.

The woman of Gujarat is a veritable abode of fun, a treasure-house of love—she is kindly spoken, experienced in intimate devices of all kinds; she has beautiful hair, a slim delicate figure; in love she quivers with excitement and is world-famous for her wantonness.

The women who come from the district of the rivers Iravati, Indus, and Satadru, between the Vipas and the Vitasta, and from the Candrabhaga can only be won [or "brought to orgasm?"] by genital kisses.

The woman of Lata becomes intensely passionate with gentle love-blows, and the use of nails and teeth—she loves embraces, is very fiery, has very delicate limbs, and dances at the prospect of the pleasure.

---

* Every textbook has a slightly different version of this gazetteer. For example:

"The women of Central India dislike wounds from nails or teeth, but enjoy kisses and love-blows. The women of the Indus region like intercourse from behind and hairpulling, those of Simhala like varied coital postures. The beauties of Maharashtra, Strirajya, and Kosala like kisses and embraces, and are specially fond of artificial penile aids. The ladies of the Carnatic like love bites and scratches, blows, intercourse stark naked, and penile devices, and are greedy for a man's sexual parts. The Dravidian girls like kisses, hairpulling, tongue- and breast-pressing, testes [?], and blows on the body. The ladies of Bengal are particularly fond of varied coital poses, kisses and embraces, love long kisses, have very tender bodies, and are devoted to pilgrimages and processions. The girls of Nepal won't stand blows or rough embraces . . . " (Smaradipika.)

How simple, to be able to proceed upon such clear-cut assumptions!

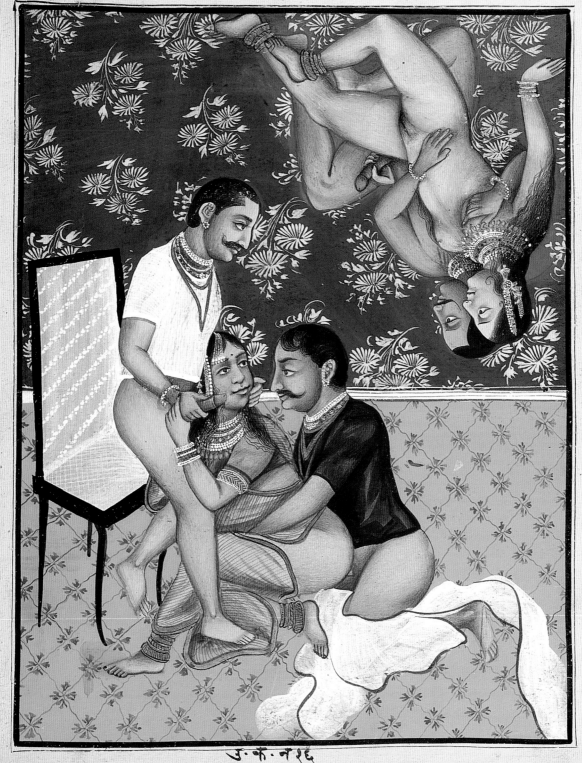

The Andhra woman oversteps the bounds of decent behavior and loves coarse manners—she becomes sick with passion, is an adept at the "mare's coitus" (vadava-ka), [gripping with the vagina or in French *le pompoir*], and is very gentle.

The women of Strirastra and Kosala can be aroused by the use of an artificial penis. They like to be struck hard, and their yoni gives vigorous twitches.

The women of Maharastra talk rudely, like peasants, are shameless, and find occasion for all the sixty-four arts of love-making. This is equally true of Pataliputra women, but they are more secretive about it.

In the Hindu erotology mutual oral sex, or "69" is known as the Crow position.

The women of Dravida can be excited by persistently stroking them, within and without, in the different forms of "outer" embrace, but respond slowly. They have a very abundant love-juice and reach complete orgasm in the very first coital embrace.

The Vanivasa (North of Kerala) women make great fun of physical defects in others, but take pleasure in concealing their own, are of moderate passion, and stand any kind of treatment.

The Lady-of-the-Buttocks from Gauda and Vanga (modern West Bengal) has a dainty, slim body, sweet voice, medium passion, a rapid walk, and no taste for love-battles.

The woman of Kamarupa (Assam, Manipur) is as delicate as a mimosa, becomes very passionate, can be excited simply by running the fingers over her, but responds fully only to the Theater of the Love-God (i.e., to her vulva); she has very pleasant speech.

The woman of Utkala (Orissa) has a passionate nature, loves tooth- and nail-play, and is delighted by genital kisses—the girls of Kalinga likewise.

The woman of Kuntala gets the greatest pleasure from all the types of nail-marking, from hard blows, and for the different techniques of genital kiss[*]—she longs for unexampled love-battles, has no inhibitions, and much passion.

(The woman of Andhra is skilled only in the bonds of love,[†] the Cola woman is refined: the Carnatic woman is clever in managing coitus; the woman of Lata likes the farfetched: the Malava woman is spiteful, the woman of Maharastra knows the Arts thoroughly—the woman of Surastra has gazelle-eyes, the woman of Gujarat speaks nicely and loves artificial devices.)[‡]

This is the teaching of the Sage (Vatsyayana) concerning local usages. A young girl from a strange part of the country should be studied accordingly: her inborn inclinations can be found only from experience—where the two conflict, personal taste is more important than local custom.

When you have considered this discrepancy between individual preference and local custom, and also body-type, speed of reaching orgasm, degree of response, age-group, and constitutional type, you can proceed accordingly—first to the appropriate "outer" and then to the "inner" forms of lovemaking. Begin with the "outer" forms —the first of these is the embrace (alingana). Here it is necessary to distinguish two types—one for use before love-play has begun, and the other for use when it is established. There are twelve manners of embracing, which we will next describe.

A man's penis should be "shaven, perfumed, and neighbor to a seemly pouch."

---

[*] The attribution of regional taste for oragenital contact is inconsistent. Vatsyayana devotes a section to oragenital intercourse—fellation is a technique practiced by feminized eunuchs, prostitutes, and homosexuals—some pandits condemn it, while others hold that "three mouths are pure, the calf's while it suckles, the dog's when he hunts, and the woman's when she makes love." Of the converse, from man to woman, and the mutual genital kiss (kakila, the Crow, or "69") he says, "for love of this, certain whores will abandon the company of upright, virtuous, and noble men of munificence, and take up with servants, base-born individuals, elephant-drivers, and the like." All forms of oragenital contact are celebrated in temple sculptures, often in a suspended position, with the man standing and the woman inverted. This emphasis reflects the Taoist-Tantric theory of the absorption of virtue from Woman, the "medicine of the Three Mountains" of Chinese alchemy. Kokkokam reinstates seven modes of auparistaka by the woman from Vatsyayana, with the recommendation that the member "should be shaven, perfumed, and neighbor to a seemly pouch."

[†] Premanibandhanaikanipuna: Probably "skilled only in the bandhas:" it could conceivably mean "skilled in erotic bondage."

[‡] Apadravyas: dildos, presumably.

of EMBRACES

(A l i n g a n a)

△ *The Mare—the technique of gripping with the vagina—is known as* **le pompoir** *in French.*

It is time now to describe the "outer" modes of love-making, beginning with embraces, of which we recognize two classes—depending upon whether the game of love has already begun or not—and in all twelve manners.

When a man meets a woman on some other errand, and contrives in so doing to touch her body, this is the embrace by touching (sprstaka).

If they walk together at a procession, or in the dark, and their bodies touch for a considerable time, this is the embrace by rubbing (udghrstaka). If one presses the other against a wall, it becomes the embrace by pressing (piditaka).

If She-of-the-Buttocks* contrives to cling to, or encompass, the man with her two breasts, while he sits or stands, so that their eyes meet, and he takes hold of her, it is the clinging embrace (viddhakajya).

For two that have not yet declared their love, there are thus four embraces by which they can make known their mind; for those who have shared love-pleasure already, the ancient authorities on our subject have recognized eight embraces by which desire may be quickened.

When the slender woman mimics the wanton tendril of a climbing plant and lassoos her lover, as a liana entangles a tree, making softly the sound "sit," giving little cries of love, and pulling down his face for a kiss, this is the liana embrace (latavestitaka).

If with sighs she stands with one foot on her lover's foot, puts the other on his hip, one arm aound his waist and the other around his shoulder, so that when he

---

★ nitambini: an epithet for a nayika resembling the Venus Callipygos (Venus of the Beauteous Buttocks) of ancient Syracuse.

kisses her she climbs as if climbing into a tree, the Founder of our subject called this the tree-climbing embrace (vrksadhirudha).* These two manners are for use when standing—the following embraces are for lovers lying together.

When the couple embrace crossing arms and thighs as if in an equal struggle, the game leads on to the "inner" forms of lovemaking, and they lie together motionless, body to body, the Founder of our subject called this the "sesame-and-rice" embrace (tilandulaka).

When the woman lies in her lover's lap or on the bed, with her face turned to his, giving him sweet and close embraces; and both press body to body heedlessly, in a storm of passion, this is the embrace known as "milk-and-water" (ksiranira).

⸹ *These sophisticated lovers make use of a popular Western sex aid— a strong chair.*

When the husband has well set the stage of the Love-God and tightly clasps the thighs, of his aroused wife between his own thighs, this is called by experts the thigh embrace (urupaghuhana).

When the woman lets fly her hair and her clothes, presses her genitals to his thighs and climbs over him to give him kisses, nail- and toothmarks, this the Founder of the subject called the pubic embrace (jaghanopaguhana).

If in her passion she presses hard into the breast of her lover, letting him feel the weight of her own breasts, it is the breast embrace (stanalingana).

When the couple set mouth to mouth, eye to eye, so that their breastbones strike together, this is the sternal embrace (lalatika).

★ "Lovers risen from bed seek to have their mistress' soft arms around their neck, and the soles of her feet placed on top of their own feet— this is a special kind of kissing at dawn." (Vasanta Vilasa.)

of KISSES

(C u s a n a)

The sites prescribed for kisses are the eyes, the neck and cheeks, the gums and within the mouth, the breasts and the space between the breasts. In Lata the people also have the habit, according to their custom, of giving passionate kisses on the genitals, the region below the navel, and the armpits.

The formal kiss (nimitaka) is that given when a woman is made by force to set her lips to a man's, but remains looking straight in front of her.

The suction kiss (sphuritaka) is that in which she makes a bud of her lower lip as if she would take hold of her husband's lower lip and pull it, but does not pull it.

The thrusting kiss (ghattitaka) is when she takes her husband's lips and holds them gently with hers, covers his eyes with her hand, and thrusts her tongue a little way into his mouth.

"Her breasts are the bosses on the forehead of Kama's elephant . . . golden waterpots . . . two lotus buds . . . "

When the man, from below, takes her chin and shakes her face a little from side to side while each sucks upon the lower lip of the other, it is the wandering kiss (bhranta).

The crosswise kiss (tiryak) is a form of this, in which she is kissed in profile from the side. Both the foregoing are called pressure kisses (piditaka) when the lower lip is held with pressure—the man opens her lips with his tongue, holds her lower lip with two fingers and presses it with his teeth only so hard as to give her pleasure.

When in kissing the man bites the upper lips, this is the upper lip kiss (uttarostha). When in a kiss given by husband to wife, or wife to husband if he be cleanshaven,

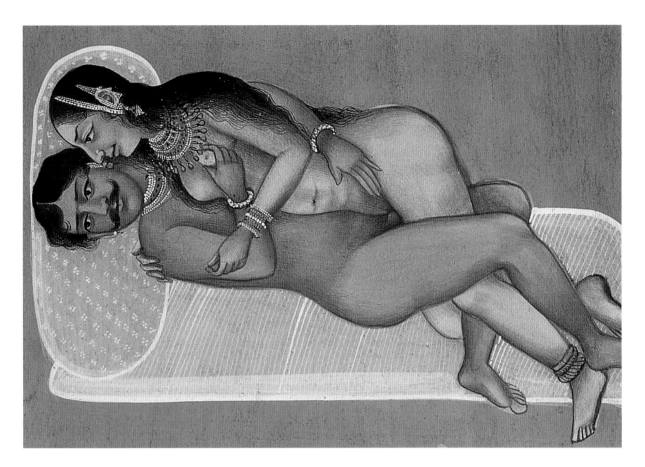

both lips of one are taken and pressed between both lips of the other, it is the closed

kiss (samputa). This becomes tonguewrestling (jihvayuddha) [French kissing]* when

their two tongues meet and struggle with each other.

High-born patrons often had their lovemaking recorded by court painters.

   As for kisses other than on the mouth, upon any of the prescribed places they may

be light, medium, pressing, or heavy.

   When the husband comes home late and kisses the woman sleeping, or pretending

to sleep, these are the two varieties of the awakening kiss.

   Another manner of kiss is the picture-kiss, given by proxy to a portrait, a mirror,

etc. This is proper to man or woman, and is used to declare a new love.

   Embracing a child or a statue as indications of desire are examples of the trans-

ferred kiss (samkranta).

* Padmasri in the Nagarasarvasva (see p.52) gives also three special tongue kisses—the needle (suci) when it is inserted pointwise in the woman's mouth, pratata when it is broadened inside like a leaf, and kari, when it is made to quiver.

of LOVE–MARKS

(Nakhacchedya)

On the armpits, the arms, the thighs, the pubic region, the breasts and neck, a couple of fiery disposition will make nailmarks.[*] Nailmarks are also made by less passionate couples, especially at first coitus, when making up a quarrel, after menstruation, when they have been drinking, or when they are about to be separated (by a journey or some other cause). The nails of passionate lovers should have large, strong tips; they should be allowed to grow but not to become dirty—they are pliant, shining, and free from ridges or cracks.[†]

A light touch on the cheek or between the breasts, given with all five nails, enough to leave a faint line and set the hairs on end, is called acchurita (the "click") from the sound "cata-cata" produced as the fingernails strike the thumbnail.

▲ *One of a series of thirty-two sexual postures featuring both Krishna and Radha.*

► *The life and lover of raja.*

A curved line (ardhacandra, ardhendu) is the half-moon; two of these drawn face to face were called by the chief authority (Vatsyayana) the circle (mandalaka), and he prescribes its use on the upper pubic region, the hollows of the loins, and the thighs. A definite scratch two or three thumb-breadths long is the line (rekha).

---

[*] "The 'dot' on your lip, the 'necklace' on your neck, the 'hare-jump' on your breast—one may see, o beauty, that your lover knows the literature of the flower-arrowed God!" (Ksemendra.)

[†] "The finest such nails are found among the Gauda people (Bengali), who do not scratch, but only touch with them. The southerners, who scratch really hard, have short, strong nails which will stand up to such use." (Yasodhara.)

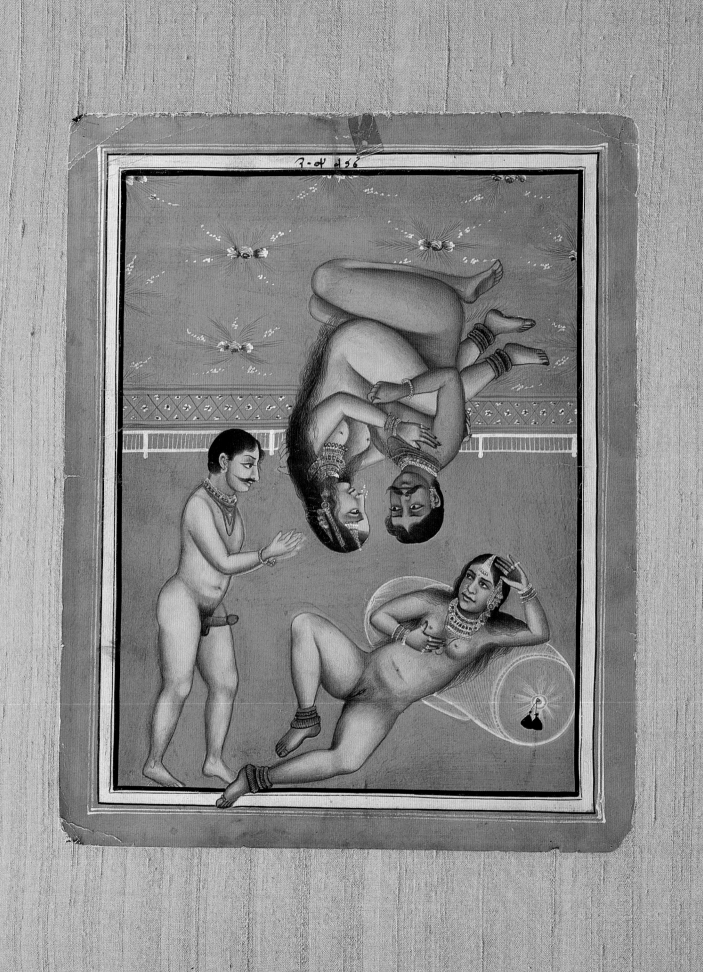

▲ Breasts are a favorite site for love bites and markings.

The peacock-foot (mayurapadaka) is made by putting the thumbnail below the nipple, the fingers above, and drawing them together to meet at the areola. The hare-jump (sasaplutaka) is made by catching the breast around the nipple with all five nails together. A scratch on the breast or the girdle-path (strip which the girdle covers) is called from its shape the lotus-leaf (utpalapattraka). Three or four deep scratches on the pubic region or the breasts are prescribed by the experts before parting on foreign travel, as a keepsake.*

---

* "When a woman sees such a mark on an intimate part of her body, an old love suddenly becomes new. . . . Such marks must never be made on another man's betrothed, however. Special marks as keepsakes or to heighten passion should only be made on covered parts of the body" (Vatsyayana)—usually the "girdle-path" or under the arm, in Temple sculpture. On the visible parts (Kandarpacudamani) "the sight of such marks worn by a beautiful young girl make even a complete stranger wishful."

OF TOOTH-MARKING *(Dasanacchedya)*

Teeth should be polished, sharp-edged, neither too large nor too small, of good color, even, and without gaps between them. They may be applied to all the sites prescribed for kisses, except the inside of the mouth and the eye.

The hidden bite (gudhaka) is a small red mark, especially on the lower lip. The swollen bite (ucchunaka) is made by pressure, on the lip or the left cheek. A longer pressure in these places produces what is called "stone against coral" (pravalamani).

The dot (bindu) is a small round wound, about the size of a sesame grain, made on the lip with two teeth only. When a mark is made by all of the teeth it is known as the necklace, or row of dots. This necklace is used by lovers as an ornament for the armpit, between the breasts, the neck, or the groin (bindumala).

A mark like an irregular circle made on the soft part of the breasts with all the teeth is called the broken cloud (khandabhraka). A long deep double row of prints with a dark-red bruise between them, proper to the convexity of the breasts, is the boar-mark (varahacarvitaka).*

★ "If, when he cannot get his own way, the man bites or scratches her, she should not suffer it, but should pay him back double—for the Dot a proper reply is the Necklace, for the Necklace the Broken Cloud. She should fight back and pretend to be enraged. If he takes her by the hair, she should fix her mouth to his when he offers it, hold him tightly, and as if drunken with love, bite him here and there. If he rests his head on her breasts and offers his neck, she should give him the Necklace and the other marks she knows.

"Next day she will smile in secret when she sees her lover publicly wearing the marks that she has made, but she will frown and scold him when he makes her show the marks upon herself.

"Two people who are so embarrassed by their mutual passion will not see their love decay, even in a hundred years!" Vatsayayana, Kama Sutra.

# of COITION and
the VARIOUS COITAL POSTURES

(Bandhas)

▶ *The posture known as jrmbhitaka or "gaping."*

▼ *A nineteenth-century carved ivory comb.*

THE PREPARATION

The proficient lover receives in a brightly lit room filled with flowers; incense is burning; he wears his most handsome clothes and has all his retinue present. He sets his lady, adorned with all her jewels, on his left, and begins a lively conversation with her. Presently he puts his left arm gently around her; he keeps contriving to touch the edge of her dress, her hands, her breasts, and her girdle; he starts singing her cheerful songs. When he sees that her desire is awakening, he sends the rest of the company away. He begins to kiss her repeatedly on the forehead, chin, cheeks, and the tip of her nose. He presses her gums and tongue with his own, making the sound "sit" continually, and implants the "click" (acchurita) nailmark on the area just below the navel, on her breasts, and on her thighs, and loosens her girdle as soon as she gains confidence, taking care that she has no chance to lose the boldness she has gained. If she shows displeasure, he kisses the lobes of her ears, presses the tip of his penis against the house of the Love-God, puts his mouth to hers, holds her tightly around the body with both arms, and finally plays the game of groping in her yoni with his hands.

DESCRIPTION OF THE YONI

In woman the house of the Love-God is of four kinds: smooth within like a lotus, covered with small knots, wrinkled, or rough like a cow's tongue. Each of these is softer and responds more quickly than the next.

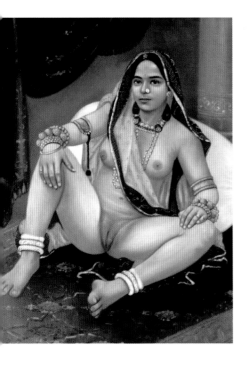

A portrait of a courtesan painted during the Raj.

The vulva contains a tube shaped to the penis, which is the swing in which the Love-God rides. Opened with two fingers, it causes the love-juice to flow—this tube and the sunshade of the Love-God (vagina and clitoris) are the two organs characteristic of Woman. The Sunshade of the Love-God is a nose-shaped organ placed just above the entrance of the God's dwelling, and is full of the veins that secrete the juice of love. Not far from it, within the vulva, is a duct purnacandra (full moon), which is filled with this juice [Bartholin's duct?]. There is also another vascular area [the vestibule?]: when these three zones are rubbed with the finger, the woman is brought into condition.

From among various named varieties of such fingerplay,* I will mention only the following: that of the Elephant's Trunk, that of the Snake-coil, the half-moon (ardhendu†), and the goad of Kama (Madanankhusa).

THE CONDUCT OF INTERCOURSE

A difficult girl can be roused by strongly stimulating the anterior blood-vessel‡ with the thumb and finger for as long as is necessary. When the kingdom of the Love-God has been fully prepared by the help of nail- and toothmarks, kisses, embraces, and fingerplay, one can proceed to the use of the penis.

---

* According to the Kokkokam, these are: karikara—with the second, third, and fourth fingers, keeping the thumb and index closed

kamayudha—with the middle and little fingers joined to the thumb

kamausadha—with the middle and little, joined in the shape of a crescent moon

madanankhusa—with ring and middle fingers

manmathapataka—with middle and little fingers

stotra—little finger only.

The Indian lover normally uses more than one finger at a time. Padmasri (see p.52) gives a different series: karana (index finger only), kanaka (index behind middle finger), vikana (middle behind index), pataka (both together, extended), trisula (index, middle and ring, trident-wise).

† "Insertion of a curved finger in the vulva."

‡ The vestibule, not the clitoris.

THE METHODS OF SEXUAL INTERCOURSE

When he has given the "outer" embraces in the approved manner and sees that his wife is inflamed, the husband will penetrate her with a weapon that should be commensurate to her parts.

By lying with the thighs together, a wide yoni can be made tighter—if it is too tight, by lying with her thighs apart she can open it. For a "low" connection (nicarata), she must in taking her pleasure close a yoni that is too large—for the "high" form (uccarata) she needs to widen it, and for an even connection (samarata) she will let it be.

The sage Vatsyayana has designated five manners of carnal copulation, namely supine (uttanaka), lateral (tiryak), seated (asitaka), standing (sthita), and prone (anata). I will now recount in full the various forms of these. Of the many uttanaka-bandhas two are prescribed for samarata, three for uccarata, and four for nicarata; but for the following the Sage made no rule.

If the woman lies on her back with the man upon her, both her legs being between his thighs, it is the country manner (gramya) and the town manner (nagaraka) if her legs are outside his.[*]

If she rests her buttocks on her hands, raising her yoni, and positions her heels outside her hips, while her lover holds her by the two breasts, it is utphullaka (the open flower).

If she raises both legs obliquely, spreading her yoni wide to let him in, it is called jrmbhitaka (gaping).

---

[*] "If the woman locks her thighs around her lover, this is the position known as ratipasa (the noose of Rati). Ratipasa is much loved by passionate women." (Smaradipika.)

In Weckerle's system, all the different postures derived from the "usual" face-to-face position by leg raising, leg crossing, etc., are treated as variants. These distinctions make up a large number of the Indian bandhas—in view of the striking differences in sensation between them, the Indian view here appears the more practical. Flanquette and cuissade positions (half-front and half-back postures with one partner astride a single leg of the other) do not seem to figure in the classical Sanskrit canon at all, though they are common in picturebooks from the eastern province of Orissa, and must surely have been as much used in India as by Western lovers today.

Lovers move from one bandha (position) to the next in the manner of dance steps.

If she sets his legs equally to her sides, while grasping his sides with her knees, this device, to be learned only by practice, is called Indra's wife[*] (Indranika).

If both in coition keep their legs extended, it is samputaka[†] (the box), of which there are two forms according to whether the woman lies on her back or on her side.

If further, she presses her extended thighs tightly together, it is piditaka (the squeeze) and if she crosses them, vestitaka (the clasp).

If the man remains still, and she "swallows" the penis with the lips of her yoni, it is the mare's coitus (vadavaka).

If she presses her thighs tightly together, raises them, and embraces them firmly, it is bhugnaka (the curved), and if she places her two soles to his chest, it becomes urah-spnutana (chest-splitting)—if one foot is extended, it is termed "the half-squeeze" (ardhanapidata).

If both the woman's legs are laid on the man's shoulders, it is the jrmbhitaka manner.[‡] If one leg is kept down and extended, it is the outstretched manner (sarita); this, if carried out with frequent alternation of the legs, becomes the celebrated "reedsplitting" (venuvidarita). If one leg is kept down and the other foot placed on the man's head, it is the spearthrust[¶] (sulacitaka).

---

[*] Or the "lock" according to Yasodhara. Indra is the god of locks and puzzles.

[†] In the version given by Smaradipika, the man kneels.

[‡] In other textbooks, this form of it is called samapada, kakapada, (crowfoot), or nagapada (elephant-foot).

[¶] He is "impaled," as seen from behind, her extended leg being the spearshaft, and the point, her other foot, coming out at the top of his head. There are several more of these closely similar semi-lateral, or foot-raising positions; another name is venika ("the man puts one of the woman's feet to his breast, the other on the bed. Other related positions are viparitaka (one foot held by the man, the other on his shoulder—Smaradipika) and ekapada (one foot held by the man, the other on the ground, while she holds him around the neck). In Smaradipika (see p.43) this is to be performed lying down—in Dinalapanika Sukasaptati it is a standing position. "If the man stands on his own feet, and holds up both the woman's feet, it is Kulisa (the thunderbolt)" Smaradipika. Traivikrama (the tripod) is given in Ananga Ranga as another name for sulacitaka; in the Pancasayaka it is a different, semi-standing position—"the man stands on his own feet, places one foot of the woman on the ground," i.e., in a backward-bent handstand on one foot and two hands, a much more difficult matter. The Nagarasarvasva has a hanupadabandha in which the woman's feet are raised to her chin—in Ratimanjari this is called utkantha, the throat position.

If putting her soles together, the woman lays both feet to the man's navel, it is the crab (karkataka).

If in the same position she thrusts violently with her feet, then it is transformed into the swing (prenkha).

If she lays each foot on the opposite thigh, it is padmasana (the lotus seat) or the half-lotus (ardhapadmasana) if only one foot is crossed.

If she passes her arms under her knees and around her neck, and her lover then holds her tightly about the neck, passing his arms between hers, it is known to experts as the cobra-noose (phanipasa).

If the girl lays her fingers to her big toes and the man, slipping his arms under her knees, clasps her around the neck, it is the trussed position (samyamana).

▲ Western lovers experiment with a "lie-back" position in a neoclassical painting from the German school.

If he then takes her, setting mouth to mouth, arm to arm, and leg to leg, it is the tortoise (Kaurma).

If finally she raises her thighs, keeping them tightly together, and he presses them with (between) his feet, it is (a form of) piditaka.*

These are the frontal positions (uttanaratas). I now go on to describe the tiryak (lateral) positions.

---

* The "advanced" positions in this section appear to be based on hatha-yoga gymnastics. The account of the tortoise (kaurma) position presents some difficulties: these more complicated bandhas do not figure in Vatsyayana. Kaurma is here given as a lying (uttana) bandha—in all other textbooks it is classed as upavista (seated). The simplest interpretation is that shown in some Indian pictures and in Temple reliefs, which accords with the definition, "mouth to mouth, arm on arm, leg on leg." But the basic position is the quite different hatha-yoga posture known as the tortoise (uttana-kaurmakasana): in this, the arms are passed through the knees and around the neck, but with the legs crossed in the lotus position.

Ananga Ranga and Kamaprabodha give three related postures to the position mentioned above:

(1) Bhandurita ("bound"); in which both partners pass arms through knees and around their own necks.

(2) Phanipasa—unclear, but they apparently pass arms around each others' necks.

(3) Kaurmaka—described as "mouth to mouth, arm on arm, leg on leg: this becomes parivartita if the woman raises her legs erect."

Dinalapanika Sukasaptati has another "close" tortoise-position "when the man puts both feet to the girl's breasts and both her feet on his shoulders, and they hold hands"—in effect a "closed" and sitting version of the more familiar European position in which, starting with the woman sitting astride, both partners lie back until they are flat, pubis to pubis, with the man's feet to the woman's breasts and her feet on his shoulders.

The names of bandhas, beside being inconsistent, do not always indicate any connection with yogic asanas of the same name.

The rather hazardous unsupported "knee-elbow" position.

If the man's thighs are placed between the woman's, this was called by the sages samudga (the chest), and if in the course of it, either partner turns away from the other (a trick that requires practice), it is parivartanaka (the turn–away).

Seated positions (asitaka-bandhas). If man and woman sit facing each other, each with one leg extended and the other drawn up, it is the two-footed position (yugmapada).[*]

If the man sits between the forearms of a beautiful woman and takes her by repeatedly shaking his thighs, it is the friction (vimarditaka) position, which becomes markatika (the monkey position) if she faces the opposite way.[†]

These are the regular forms of copulation. I will now deal separately with the "picture" positions (citramohana).

When a couple stands up, leaning for support against a wall, a pillar, or a tree (sthita—standing—positions), there are four modes of proceeding. If the man passes his arms under the girl's knees and raises her for penetration, while she puts her arms around his neck, it is the knee-elbow position (janukurpura), the name being a compound of "knees" and "elbow."

If (only) one leg is raised, it is Hari's step[‡] (harivikrama).

If she places her two soles in his two hands while he leans back for support against the wall, it is the two-sole position (dvitala).

---

[*] Each extends the same (right or left) leg, and locks the other behind the partner's back.

[†] She sits or kneels astride his lap; he leans back on his hands with his legs extended and raises himself off the ground. The most popular sitting position (with the woman astride, legs about the waist), the sitting-form called in Ananga Ranga kirti (the glory), is missing here, but occurs in Konarak temple, and in Nagarasarvasva (see p.52), where it is called lalita-bandha. Far more remarkable than the inclusion of unusual positions is the exclusion of such common ones. The absence of all the flanquette and cuissade positions has already been noted.

[‡] The reference is to the Strides of Vishnu (Hari) when he encompassed the universe. He is usually shown standing on one foot and raising the other above his head.

[¶] Probably for reasons of design, standing positions are by far the most common citrarata or "picture-positions" in temple art. It is odd that the detailed accounts of citrarata in the erotic textbooks miss out a great many of the most common sculptural bandhas. Yet the omitted postures recur perpetually in different temples. This is all the more puzzling because of the zeal with which Hindu art usually adheres to specification: secular poets were heavily censured by commentators for describing lovers' embraces that did not square with the rules of Classical erotology.

If she sits in his hands with her arms around his neck and her legs around his waist, moving herself by putting the toes of one foot against the wall, throwing herself about, crying out, and gasping continually, this is the suspended position (avalambitaka).[¶]

In the vyanata positions, the woman goes down on all fours, like an animal, and her lover, entering from behind, puts his weight on her like a bull.

If she puts her palms on the ground, tucks in her head, and moves slowly forward when he has mounted her, while he remains upright, bull-fashion, it is called the cow (dhenuka or in Arabic, el houri).

In the elephant position (aibha), he holds his penis in his hand and leaps her, like a bull elephant, while she lays her brow, face, and breasts to the ground and raises her buttocks.[*]

There are other modes of copulation described that imitate the dog, the gazelle, and the camel.[†]

The core content of the erotic textbooks predates the age of the temple builders.

PLURAL INTERCOURSE *(samghataka)*

If one man has connection at once with two women, whose thighs are laid opposite ways,[‡] or a passionate girl enjoys two lovers at once, this is called plural intercourse.

There is yet another manner of it by which one woman may enjoy four men, or one man four women. This is accomplished by giving nail- and toothmarks and by genital contact, using hands, feet, mouth, and linga simultaneously.

These are the rules, then, for managing the "picture" positions.

....

[*] She should also alternatively draw up and extend her legs, according to Dinalapanika Sukasaptati, which gives all the other (little-differing) animal-bandhas in full.

[†] Nagarasarvasvra has vyaghravaskanda, the tiger-spring—the woman lies on her face holding her ankles behind her and the man kneels, raising her thighs onto his knees and holding her waist. The name is due to the "broken-backed appearance of a quadruped seized in mid-spine by a tiger."

[‡] "One with the linga, the other with the finger or tongue." (Kancinatha.) Chinese texts give postures of this kind for alternate vaginal penetration of four women.

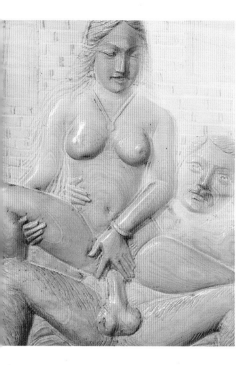

▲ An ivory carving showing marked Western influence.

Some books* have given special names to the different manners of moving the penis in the vagina (churning, pressing, the boar-thrust, and so on), but these I have omitted as unprofitable. The pressing, striking, or rubbing of the yoni can be conducted in three ways—from above, centrally, or from below. If the Lady-of-the-Buttocks proves insatiable, then her lover may hold a lingam in his hand.†

THE SIGNS OF SATISFACTION IN WOMAN

When the girl begins to close her eyes, her lover should clasp her more tightly. Limpness, eye-closing, and swooning are the signs of enjoyment.‡ She will move her yoni repeatedly, give the sound "sit," lose all shyness, and be beside herself with love—this is the point at which her feeling is most intense.

The signs of dissatisfaction by contrast are these: she threshes her arms about, strikes out, will not let go of the man, and suddenly throws herself upon him.

....

* These other books include the Kama Sutra itself. Vatsyayana has a section devoted to male movements (purusopasrptaka) as follows (see also Rati-ratnapradipika):

"Straightforward penetration is called upasrptaka. If the man takes his penis in his hand and gives it a rotary movement, this is mundhana (churning). If he lowers his pubis and strikes upward, it is the stab (hula). The reverse stroke from above downward, to be given very forcibly, is the rub (avamardana). If he penetrates deeply and maintains a long, steady, forward pressure, it is piditaka (the pressure stroke). If he withdraws a long way and then returns with a sharp thrust, it is nirghata (the gust). A powerful stroke given to one side is vaharaghata (the boar-stroke)—the same on each side successively is the ox stroke (vrsaghata, i.e., with two horns). Three or four sharp strokes with no withdrawal between them is the sparrow game (chatakavilasita). Finally the 'box' (samputa) is the action that is called 'the end of lust.'"

† Presumably an artificial phallus (apadravya). Yasodhara drily explains the inclusion of metal-work and lathe-turning among the subsidiary arts prescribed in the Kama Sutra for a liberal feminine education by the need to manufacture these. The devices described by Vatsyayana include both dildos and penile prostheses (rings, sheaths, and erection-maintainers similar to the modern Japanese kabutogata). They were to be used in satisfying very demanding women, in the "high" mode of coitus to remedy disproportion, and by kings with obligations to a numerous harem in excess of their physical powers—they were also locally popular in certain districts. Under the same heading, Vatsyayana mentions the various forms of ampallang and the piercing of the glans to accommodate them, a custom once confined to Malays and Kayans, but now enjoying a vogue among body piercing enthusiasts in the West.

‡ "Listen, friend, to a story about my fool of a lover. When I shut my eyes in the final ecstasy, he thought I was dead, took fright, and let go of me!" (Kuttani-mata.)

"With horripilation on her breasts, crushed now in a strong embrace, with the cloth on her fair buttocks wet with her glutinous love-juice, babbling piteously 'No, no, darling—that's enough!' is she asleep, or dead, or has she vanished into my heart?" (Vasanta Vilasa.)

INVERSE POSITION *(purusayita)*

When the whim takes her, or when her lover is tired, the woman can carry out inter-course after the male fashion. She will act the man's part, either by turning him over after intromission has taken place[*] or from the start of intercourse.

If when astride him she bends her legs and makes a rotary movement, it is bhramara[†] (the wheel)—if she moves from side to side, it is prenkholita (the swing) made up from prenkha and ulita. She strikes[‡] him and cries "sit;" she laughs and says boldly. "Now, you coward, I've got you down and it is I who will make you die. Hide yourself, haven't I shamed your pride?" So striking him continually, her bracelets jingling, her hair falling on his lips, and her thighs shuttling back and forth in an ecstasy, she will cease only with her climax. When the man sees that she is tiring, he will turn her over and finish in the "box" (samputa) position. If she is still not satis-fied, he should perform angulirata, finger-intercourse. A woman who has just finished a menstrual period,[¶] or who has lately borne her first child, should not use the viparita (purusayita) position, and it is said that a pregnant woman, a harini (mrgi), and one who is fat, or very slim, or a young girl, should avoid it.

---

[*] The variants here are not bandhas but rather movements. The corresponding obverse position, depicted in the erotic sculpture at the temple of Konarak with the woman astride facing the man's feet, seems to be missing from Indian literary erotology. Dinalapanika Sukasaptati gives other purusayita positions; matsya (fish): "the man lies outspread— the woman lies on him closely with her feet on his two legs and her breasts pressed to his chest;" hamsa, in which the man sits half-erect on the woman's joined feet; and dolita (swing) in which he draws his feet up to his chest, and she lies with her belly on his soles, being lifted and swung on them, "while they both hold hands and she pretends to be frightened." Smaradipika gives two positions: "If the woman lies flat on the man's two thighs, holds her feet (behind her back) with both hands, and vigorously moves her hips, this is hamsalilaka (the duck or swan game). If she sits astride the penis with both soles on the ground and her hands over her breasts, it is the play-seat (lilasana)."

[†] Probably she moves her pelvis only. Dinalapanika Sukasaptati has a more energetic "wheel" position (Cakrabandha) in which she turns on the penis as an axle, lying face down on the supine man, and working around with her hands. Rotary positions of this sort are easy and rewarding.

[‡] Ananga Ranga gives four strokes to be used by the woman—with the fist on the chest (santanita), with the flat of the hand (pataka), with the thumb only (bindumala), and with the angle of the thumb and forefinger (kundala), the last being especially excitant.

[¶] The risk is that she will conceive in this position and the fetus will not know whether to adopt a male or a female role (Yasodhara).

of LOVE–BLOWS *and*
LOVE–CRIES

(P r a h a n a n a   a n d   S i t k r t a)

THE STRIKING OF BLOWS *(Prahanana)*

It has been said that "love is a tussle, in which both are blinded by passion." It is not surprising then that the striking of blows has a part to play in it, as does the uttering of cries.

Love-blows (prahanana) are struck with the palm, the back of the hand, the clenched hand, or the whole hand outspread—on the back, the sides, the pubic region, between the breasts, and on the head, which are the stations of love.

LOVE-CRIES *(Sitkrta)*

The sound "Him", a sound like thunder, the sounds "sut," "dut," "phut," gasps, moans, and cries of "Stop!" "Harder!" "Go on!" "Don't kill me!" and "No!" have the generic name of sitkrta.[*] Little shrieks that variously resemble the cry of the heron, dove, Indian cuckoo,[†] hamsa, and peacock can be evoked by love-blows, but are described by the experts of carnal copulation as being heard at other times, too.[‡] The sound "Him" epresents a sudden expulsion of breath from the nose and throat and the thundering (shuddering) sound, which is made in the same way, resembles the collision of storm clouds. The sound "dut" is like the snapping of a hollow stalk—the sound "phut" is like a berry dropping into a jar of water.

▶ *The various rear-entry positions are notoriously difficult to identify.*

---

[*] "Sit"-crying: the response to an erotic touch, a gasp in through nearly closed teeth. The "thunder" sound is a shuddering expiratory gasp. Some ladies cry "Mother!" as Vatsyayana reminds us—the wife of "The Leopard" in di Lampedusa's novel screamed "Gesumaria!" at the critical moment.

[†] Kokila or Kakila: its voice is a series of whoops, rising in pitch as the song continues.

[‡] "Sitkrta is perfectly in order even when no blows are struck." (Ratirahsyadipika.) Indian literature often refers to them, and to the competence with which birds, especially parrots and mynahs, which learn best in the dark, can imitate them, thus obtaining an embarrassing party piece.

THE USAGE OF LOVE-BLOWS AND LOVE-CRIES

According to the teaching, striking with the back of the hand between the breasts evokes the moaning sound. The back should be struck with the knuckles, and the head with the hand bent into the shape of a cobra's hood, while blows on the sides and genitals are given with the flat of the hand.* "The shears," and other types of striking which are used in the South are reprobated by the Masters.†

▲ *The West's influence is evident not only in the figurative style of this painting (produced during the Raj), but also in the variety of pigments available to the artist.*

With the girl sitting on his knee, the lover should strike her on the back with one fist. She will pretend to be angry and retaliate, screaming, gasping, and becoming drunken with love. Toward the end of intercourse, he will strike very gently and continuously over the heart of the girl while she is still penetrated, and at each stroke she will give the cry of "sit." If she tussles with him, he will strike on her head with the curved hand, and in response she will give the sounds of "kat" and "phut" and will gasp or moan. Just before orgasm he will strike quickly repeated blows with the flat of the hand on her genital and her sides. If her passion begins to wane, the Lady-of-the-Buttocks will utter cries like those of the quail or "hamsa." After her climax she may again scream or gasp repeatedly. At other times, too, a woman will utter love cries that make her infinitely desirable, without being either in pain or weary of intercourse.

* "Striking is of four kinds—with the hollow hand, the back of the hand, the fist, and the flat of the hand, four manners. The sites for it are as follows—with the flat on sides and genitals, with the fist on the back, further on the head and face with the hollowed hand held like a snake-hood, and over the heart with the back of the hand. If the woman is hurt and hits her man with the fist on his chest, this is termed by the adepts samtanika; if in intercourse she slaps him with the flat palm, it is a pataka; a blow with the thumb only is bindu (the dot). If the woman in excessive passion strikes slowly with thumb and middle finger together (? pinching), it is kundula (the ornament)." (Ananga Ranga.)

† The "shears," "wedge," etc., are mudras or hand-positions used in striking. They are described by Yasodhara, being quoted for condemnation by Vatsyayana, together with a number of accidents due to their use: "In Southern girls one can see the mark left on the breast by the 'wedge' . . . this is a barbarous practice, however, and should be abandoned, says Vatsyayana. It is also dangerous. With the 'wedge' the King of Kola accidentally killed the hetaira Citrasena during love-play. The Kuntala Satakarni killed Queen Malayavati in the same way, with the 'shears.' while Naradeva, who had a paralyzed hand, put out the eye of a dancing girl by misaiming a blow with the 'needle.'"(Kama Sutra.)

Burton and Arbuthnot assumed that the names must refer to carpenters' tools. The sadistic tastes of Southerners are condemned in Sanskrit texts, but the idea of "instruments" being used appears to be a blunder. The Kokkokam omits this aspersion for its Tamil-speaking Southern readers, substituting "but the oversexed women of Pandya are hard nuts to crack—one can pound on their breasts with stone balls and still get nowhere."

Passion and roughness in copulation, combined with tenderness, usually make only the man attractive, but according to local and other customs a short exchange of roles, from passion, can be delightful.

When a spirited horse reaches a full gallop, it takes no heed of obstacles: so two lovers in the struggle of love take no heed for blows, knocks, or Death itself. But it is the duty of the man to consider the tastes of women, and to be tough or tender entirely in conformity to his beloved's wishes.*

▲ Pleasing his partner, is required of the Indian lover.

ORAL INTERCOURSE

The Sage (Vatsyayana) has dealt fully with this matter. To his account who would be so rash as to add anything?†

---

* Vatsyayana has a section on the end of intercourse that is worth including for its own sake, as a tailpiece to this section:

"When both are satisfied, they will suddenly become embarrassed—they will go separately to wash without looking at each other, as if they were strangers. When they come back, they will have lost their embarrassment—they will sit down again as before, side by side, and take betel, and he will rub sandalwood or sweet oil on her skin. Putting his left arm around her, he should hold the cup for her to drink, while they converse pleasantly together. They will take water, sherbet, or whatever else their fancy and habit chooses—fruit juice, soups, sour-rice broth, roast meats, mango, dried meat, and lemon juice with sugar, according to the custom of the district. He will taste the dishes and tell her which are sweet, which are mild, and which are plain. Or they will go and sit on the roof in the moonlight, and he will hold a suitable discourse with her. If she lies in his lap looking up at the moon, he will tell her names of the constellations and show her the Southern Cross, the Pole Star, and the crown of seven stars in the Great Bear. This is the manner of concluding sexual intercourse." (Kama Sutra.)

† For the contentious matter so expertly avoided here, see note to p.83. Other texts list additional pleasures. To the stylized mignrardizes given by Kokkoka (nailmarks, toothmarks, blows, and cries), the Ananga Ranga and Pancasayaka add hair-pulling (kesagraha) "to be done very slowly," to heighten passion and draw the beloved's face to the lover for kissing. The Smaradipika adds mardana (which includes both pressing and the tickling erotic massage known in France as *les pattes d'araignee*) "on both arms, both breasts, vulva, and navel—six sites in all" and nectar-drinking (ras-apana) "at breasts, lips, mouth, tongue, and nipples—five sites in all."

According to the Nagarasarvasva, the varieties of pressure (mardanam) are adipitam (squeezing with the whole hand), sprstakam (touching with the palms), kampitakam (repeated quick pressure in the same place), and samakrama (repeated squeezing of different places). The varieties of holds (grahama) are baddha-musti (in the closed fist), vestitakam (twining the hair), krtagranthika (interknotting the fingers), and samakrsti (pinching).

To these manipulations some of the poets add shampooing or massage of the woman's body to prevent stiffness after acrobatic intercourse.

the WOOING OF A BRIDE

(Kanyavisrambhanam)

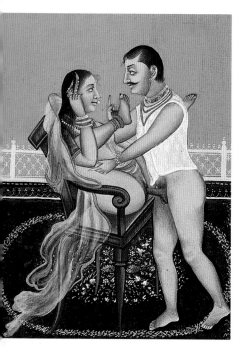

▲ "Women's bodies are as
soft as flowers . . . "

► "If she is not brought
to experience true love,
through this state of anxiety
she may come to hate men
in general . . . "

CHOOSING A BRIDE

Respectable men, who follow the Threefold Aim in life, should marry a woman of their own social standing who has never been previously betrothed, say the sastras. Honorable persons will always avoid marriage, association, games, friendship, and the like with persons of higher or lower positions.

The rules for wooing are these: the ideal bride, to be preferred above all others, is one with a skin like a lotus-petal, or yellowish-tinted like gold, with a delicate flush to her hands, feet, nails, and eyes; well-proportioned soft feet; who eats little, sleeps little, has on her hands the marks of the Lotus, the Pitcher, and the Discus (attributes of Vishnu). She must not be red-haired or have a pendulous belly or a hanging lip.

Wily men who know the rules will avoid any girl they find out of her house, weeping or yawning, or asleep; a girl named for a mountain, a tree, a river, or a bird; one who is over- or undersized, is bent or bony, has a hanging lip, hollow or red eyes, hands and feet which are rough to the touch; one who sighs, laughs, or cries at meals; one who had inverted nipples, or a beard, or unequal breasts; one who is dwarfish, has flap-ears like winnowing fans, bad teeth, a harsh voice, spindle legs, or is scrawny; one who likes going about with male hangers-on; one who has hair on her hands, sides, chest, back, legs, or upper lip; one who makes the ground shake when she passes, or gets a crease on her cheeks when she laughs; one whose great toe is too small in proportion to the other toes, whose middle toe touches the great toe, or whose two smallest toes fail to touch the ground—all these are to be avoided in choosing a bride.

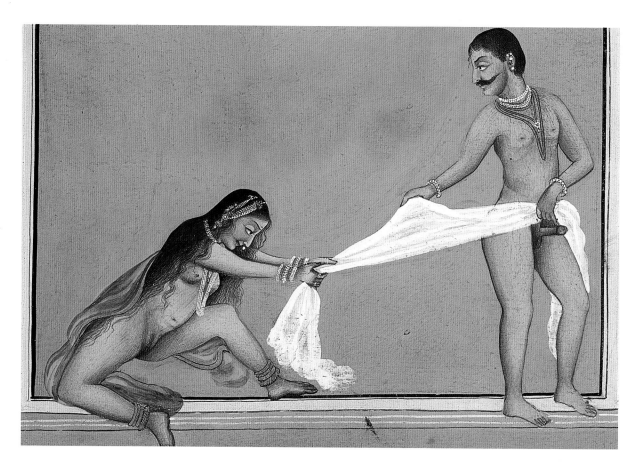

▲ *Indian erotology stresses the importance of love-games in courtship.*

OF THE WEDDING NIGHT

The bridegroom should not approach his bride on the wedding night—otherwise she will become bored during the next three nights when she has to sit and keep watch. For three days he preserves continence, and does not attempt anything presumptuously until he has first won her heart. Women's bodies are as soft as flowers—they dislike embraces that are inflicted on them by people who have not yet won their intimate regard. The wooer will first show his love for his bride through the offices of her friends, and progress slowly with her as he wins her confidence. If she is a virgin and has never been alone with him, he should operate, say the rules, in complete darkness. When the girl is at ease with him, he will very briefly embrace her with the upper half of his body. He will pass some betel from his mouth to hers, tell her he loves her, speak kindly to her, kneel to her, and adopt other such measures to please her. He can then give her a pure, tender kiss and play gentle games with her. As if unintentionally, he asks her some simple question—if she does not answer, he asks, "Do I please you, sweetheart?" She will motion with her head, not answer with words. As her confidence increases little by little, she will hide her face and smile while the bridesmaid whispers in her ear what the bridegroom told her in private— "He said such and such, and this is what he said of the joy that he has in you. . . . " she will say, including a good many lies of her own. If the bridesmaid is waggish and overplays her hand, the groom should say playfully and not over-distinctly, "I never said anything of the kind!" When she gains confidence further, the bride will ask for betel or flowers, and he will give them to her or lay them in her lap. Then he should touch the buds of her nipples with the tips of his fingers, slide his hand down to her pubis, and take it away again. If she stops him, he takes his hand away and says, "I won't do it again, if you'll put your arms around me." Once he has contrived by treating her gently to get her sitting on his knee, he will frighten her out of her wits by saying, "I'll bite and scratch your pretty face, and I'll mark myself all over and say you did it, and make you ashamed before all your friends." Then he kisses her all over, and as her bashfulness is conquered by handling he unties her girdle. Having introduced his penis in the approved manner, he amuses her until all traces of fear are removed by his gentle exertions. This road to the deep and lasting affection of young maidens I have learned from my studies of the Kama Sutra, and I tell it to you.

THE ART OF WINNING

Neither too much compliance, nor too little—with girls, a middle way brings the best result. The man who knows how best to foster woman's passion in his own beloved and how to win her heart will be her choice. A girl who is courted by a man she does not care for will be anxious, frightened, and tetchy, and will hate him forthwith. If she is not brought to experience true love, through this state of anxiety she may come to hate men in general, or be hated by them, and her suitor will turn elsewhere.

CONCERNING WIVES

(Bharyadikarikam)

OF WIFELY DUTIES

A young woman should be wholly subject to her husband and honor him with word, heart, and body, as a god.* Under his instruction she should carry out the duties of the house and make it clean and neat day by day.

She should treat elder relatives, friends, servants, and the circle of her husband's acquaintances according to the dignity of each, without arrogance or deceit. She should wear a white, simple dress for her own recreation and when entertaining, and a red and costly one for her husband's pleasure.

In the garden she should plant marjoram, three species of jasmine, patchouli, flowering and sweet-scented herbs, fruit trees, radishes, kala, gourds, acacia, and so on.

She should not converse with whores, witches, begging nuns, women who follow actors or gallants, nor with herb- and potion-sellers. She should give her husband every day the meals he desires, according to what she knows he likes, and what is good for him.

▶ *"In conversation a sage*
. . . in bed a harlot . . . "

If she hears the voice of a visitor, she should receive him, and wash both his feet. If her husband is inclined to squander his wealth, she should save it on the quiet.

---

* Karyesu dasi karnesu mantri
  rupe ka Laksmi ksamaya dharitri
  sneha ka mata sayanesu vesya
  sadkarma yukta kila dharma patni

In work a servant, in conversation a sage, in beauty as Lakshmi, in endurance as the Earth,

In care a mother, in bed a harlot—these six, they say, are the duties of a wife.

—Sanskrit proverb.

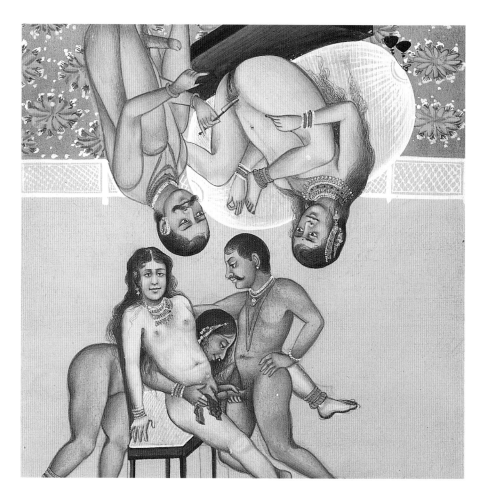

► *A painting from the series of double-headed erotic images produced in Uttar Pradesh at the turn of the century.*

She should go out only with his permission, and attended. She should go to bed after him and rise before him. She should never leave him asleep, nor interrupt him at his devotions, but share in his religious observances and his vows.

She will not loiter in corners, or at the door, nor scold. She will avoid lonely spots and huts, and not converse needlessly with any man.

In making purchases she will take proper account of prices and what is in season. She will make provision of utensils of wood, clay, leather, and metal in suitable numbers and qualities. She will keep a stock of scarce medicaments. She will keep proper accounts and regulate her spending according to income.

She will keep a sharp subversion over the use of hay, chaff, corn, wood, charcoal, and ash, the employment of servants, the rota of duties, and the reconditioning of her husband's cast-off clothes, which she will clean and issue to the servants. She will attend to the maintenance of his retinue, carts, and oxen, and the inspection of monkeys, cuckoos, parrots, mynahs, cranes, and the like.

She will obey her husband's elder relatives, control her language in dealing with them, avoid laughing at them openly, and behave with modesty.

She will treat a second wife as her sister, and a second wife's children as her own.

THE HUSBAND'S ABSENCE

When her husband is away, she should wear only her lucky ornaments[*] and live in the precepts of the gurus and Brahmins. She will have her bed at the foot of her elders',[†] spend little, inquire continually for news of her husband, take pains to forward any work he has left unfinished, and offer prayers and sacrifices for his luck and safety. If she visits relatives, she must not go alone nor stay too long. When her husband comes back safe and sound, she can go once more to a festival and offer a sacrifice.[‡]

OF POLYGAMY

If a man has more than one wife, he must be kind and tactful, without overlooking any misconduct. He must never discuss one wife's ailments, or the intimacies between them, with another wife, or repeat any jealous remarks she may make. He will not interfere in the proper sphere of the junior wives.[¶] If one of them talks of the faults of another, he will tactfully reprove her. He must give pleasure to all his beloveds, so long as they live, with walks in pleasure-gardens, love, care, and gifts.

---

[*] To show she is not a widow.

[†] Upaguru sayanam—more probably "lie chastely."

[‡] Vatsyayana gives it as one of the duties of a neglected wife (durbhaga) to find out privately if her husband is in love with another woman, and if so, tactfully bring them together. We might consider this equally the duty of the husband of a virakta—a wife who does not care for him.

[¶] take sides between them.

CONCERNING RELATIONS
with STRANGE WOMEN

(Paradarikam)

A nineteenth-century miniature of a nayika.

The last section completes in brief the subject of wives. I will now deal with the pursuit of strange women.* This is the enemy of life and of reputation and the ally of godlessness, and it should be undertaken only under the compulsion of the ten stages of love, not simply upon impulse.

Love-at-sight first, then brooding, then scheming—the loss of sleep, loss of weight, inability to concentrate, the destruction of one's sense of shame, frenzy, collapse, and finally death—these are the ten stages of love. When a man finds himself launched on this course, he is obliged to follow a strange woman to preserve his life. One can, after all, find new wives, goods, and land, beget new sons, and rebuild one's happy estate, but life is irreplaceable, and health once lost cannot be renewed.

FORBIDDEN WOMEN

According to Kokkoka, adultery is not to be undertaken lightly.

Seduction of a betrothed girl or the daughter of a Brahmin incurs lasting pollution and a daily guilt equal to that of Brahmin-murder.

---

* Strange in the sense of not one's own (svakiya). She may be someone else's wife (parakiya) or public property (sadharani). The adulteress can be of six kinds, "sly," "reckless," "conscience-stricken," "scared," "well-guarded," or "sluttish" (vidagha, mudita, anusayana, laksita, gupta, kulata), and there are at least nine named varieties of whore. After further subdivision by age and situation, it has been calculated that there were 384 possible categories of nayika, own wives included—without counting the somatotypes (mrgi, padmini, etc.) or the sattvas, which overlap. Computer dating agencies might find a modern application of this system that its authors did not foresee.

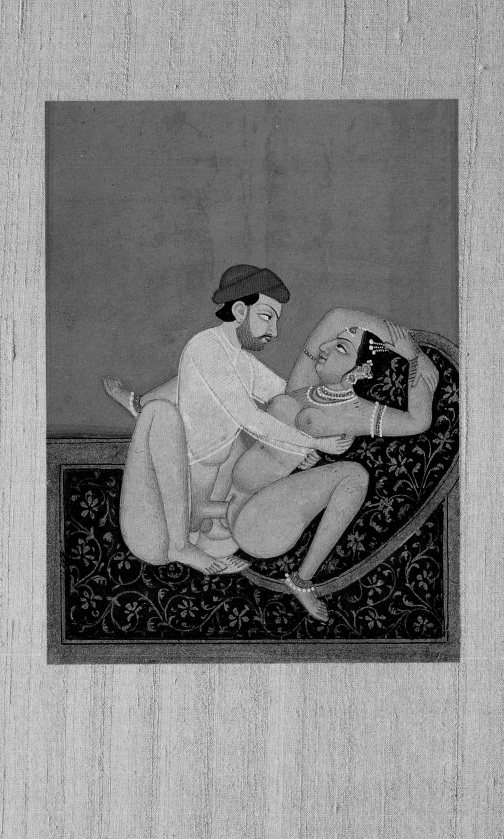

The wife of a Brahmin is not to be approached: she is not, however, absolutely to be excluded, if she has had to do with at least five men previously. This does not apply to the wives of sages,[*] friends, relations, and rulers (they should never be seduced, however promiscuous). A woman who has been put out of her caste, a personal friend, a child, a friaress, an invalid, a woman who makes love in public, a lunatic, or one who is ill-smelling, aged, unable to keep intimate secrets, red-haired,[†] very dark, or a ward of someone else, are always to be avoided as a matter of practice—but the doctors name them particularly as unsuitable for illicit affairs.

OTHER CASES IN WHICH IT MAY BE
NECESSARY TO SEEK STRANGE WOMEN

1. "Her husband is my enemy's friend. She may contrive a split between them." Or: "If she falls in love with me, she may be able to influence my enemy, who now plans to kill me."

2. "If I go to her, I shall be out of danger." Or: "She is now a condition of my existence, miserable man that I am." Or: "She knows all my faults and still loves me—but if I drop her, she may ruin me, for she may go around railing at me and saying 'this is the sort of man he is, this lover of mine!'" Or: 'If I have intercourse with her, I shall be doing a friendly service to her."

A man should not pursue a woman so from simple desire, but only for solid reasons of this kind, unless he feels himself about to go out of his mind with love, and cannot trouble further to ask for sound reasons.

---

[*] But a man may sire a child on his guru's wife by the guru's request; in fact, in ancient times he must as a duty. This is clear in the Mahabharata where Uddalaka requested a pupil to sire him a son and got Svetaketu. King Galava, wishing to give his guru a present, borrowed a princess and put her to stud to a number of heirless kings; then presented her, with the accrued stud fees, to his instructor Visvamitra. He got a rebuke for his pains—"Why did you not bring her first to me? I would have sired all four sons!"

[†] Not only for esthetic reasons—she is very likely to prove a witch (yogini) and kill her lover.

Before embarking on an affair with a strange woman, one ought seriously to weigh the possible loss of position, income, and existing love-arrangements: it is very hard to stop the march of love once it is in motion! Love for an object that can only be enjoyed at great expense, that will be hard to get rid of, and that is forbidden in any case, is bound by its nature to progress uncontrollably to some mischief or other.

LOVE AND LOVING IN MAN AND WOMAN

A woman becomes enamored on seeing a handsome man, likewise a man when he sees a handsome woman. But there is this important difference between them, that woman, once she is in love, loves regardless of convention. She will not give herself immediately to a wooer, for when she gives she does so with her whole being—a man, by contrast, conducts his love affairs with some regard to ethics, time, place, etc., whether to do or not to do. He is suspicious of a woman easily won, loves one who is hard to get, and is willing to risk taking pains over her in vain. So much for the difference between Man and Woman.

In protracted lovemaking a hookah was a useful and pleasurable diversion.

REASONS WHICH MAY MAKE A WOMAN HOLD BACK

I will now detail some considerations that may make a woman resist seduction:* Love of her husband; love of her children; fear of the consequences; in a few cases, moral scruple; constant presence of her husband; inability to bear the knowledge of her own fault; because, although she wants to keep her wooer deeply in love, she is for the moment enjoying someone else; because she does not want to see him suffer on her

★ Into an illicit love affair.

account; excessive respect for him, if he is a nayaka, or friend, or an associate of her husband; contempt for him, if he fails to notice her advances, is elderly, or her social inferior, is easily fobbed off by cunning, or has no regard to times and places; dejection at the idea that he probably makes similar advances to all his women friends, or that he does and does not know her heart; anxiety, if he is a public figure, or notoriously fickle; or for fear that her relatives may find out and repudiate her.

These are the commonly cited reasons that make a woman hold back even though enamored.

COUNTERING THESE

The first five scruples above mentioned are best quieted by stepping up the level of desire. The group of objections beginning, "I could never bear . . . " can be dispelled by showing the woman an escape route appropriate to the case. According to the Masters, over-esteem can be met by familiarity, contempt by spreading a reputation for subtlety and sexual skill, depression by polite attention, and anxiety by getting her to trust you.

OF SUCCESSFUL SEDUCERS

The most successful suitors are the following: men who can tell the tale, experts in lovemaking, the affectionate, men who can give a public performance, the robust, the cultured, those who have youth and looks, childhood playmates, partners at games or dancing, experts in storytelling and the arts, those who have previously acted as go-betweens. Also successful is one who knows a woman's intimate weaknesses, even if he has no other qualities to commend him; one who has reconciled her to a friend; one who has previously possessed a woman of qualities; one who is lovable, or of

★ In some parts of India, a sexual and jesting relationship between sister-in-law (bhauji) and her husband's younger brother (dewar) is socially acceptable. It plays a large part in folk tradition, and is presumably the last vestige of the fraternal polyandry of the *Mahabharata* (see p.43 note). By contrast, however, the elder brother-in-law is strictly taboo.

◄ The ancient sages advise a man who is regarded comtemptuously by women to create a reputation for himself of "subtlety and sexual skill."

good family, a brother-in-law,* a favorite servant, a likeminded neighbor, a stepsister's husband; one who is generous; a lover of theater; a man known to be of the "ox" type; a man who has divorced his wife for good reasons; and a man whose clothes look grand and expensive. These are the most successful seducers.

OF SEDUCERS

The following women are seducers: A woman who is always standing at the door; one who looks back at you sideways when you stare at her; one who has been thrown over and has lost her pleasures; one who is childless, and despised for lack of progeny; one who is shameless, or neglected, or who loves company; whose children have all died, who has been deserted through barrenness, or who is unjustly slighted by co-wives; a young widow, a woman who has had too many pleasures, a woman who is poor; an estimable woman who has married beneath her; an educated woman who scorns her husband; an eldest daughter with many brothers-in-law; one whose husband is traveling and who helps in her relatives' house; one who is perpetually visiting relations; one who is sociable, and has a jealous husband; one who has only daughters; a handsome woman who is wronged for some reason; a young woman who is rebuked; a woman of affectionate nature. Beside these, the wife of a strolling entertainer, a cripple, a stinkard, a bumpkin, or an invalid, or one married to a poltroon, an old man, an impotent man, or a waster—these women can be had for the asking.

▲ *Erotic miniature portraits were sometimes exchanged by lovers, like this one dating from the nineteenth century.*

OTHER OBSERVATIONS

A woman who has the second toe of her left foot longer than the big toe or shorter than the middle toe, or whose little toes do not touch the ground or the toe next to them, who squints, has yellow-gold eyes, and who smiles when she has no reason—such a one the hand-readers call pumscali—she who runs after men.

A man can be successful with women if he studies form, is familiar with their attributes, and can quiet any scruples they may have. Sexual desire springs from the natural disposition. Strengthened by experience and stimulated by intelligence, it becomes irresistible and unquenchable.

ON MAKING CONTACTS

Women who speak frankly and who openly show their willingness from the outset can be wooed personally; contrary women should be approached through a go-between.

In the personal approach, one should start by getting the woman's friendship without betraying other intentions.

Next, use your glance as a go-between and a love-letter, and send it often in her direction. Keep adjusting your hair, tap with your fingernails, rattle your ornaments, press your lips together.

When you sit on a companion's knee, yawn, rub your limbs, speak stammeringly, and keep twitching an eyebrow.

Make remarks, nominally about other matters, that could also refer to her, listen intently to her when she speaks, and express your desire in hints.

Embrace a friend or a child over-affectionately. Pretend to fondle her children on her knee and in doing so contrive to touch her body. Give toys to these same children, and having so made contact with their mother, strike up an acquaintance.

Keep dropping in upon her, so that the people of the house get to know and like you. Tell her equivocal and significant love-stories, to which she will probably listen unsuspecting.

Once you have quickened her love, give her a clear token—in this frequent, or even daily, intimacy, take an opportunity to put an arm around her.

Set her on a basis of intimacy with your own wife. When she has something to buy or sell, assist her to arrange it—throw dust in the eyes of the other party, and so establish an obligation between you.

Stage a dispute with her or her folk over some fact or question of history, make a wager on it, then call to ask her the result.

Having won her friendship by these means, you watch for her signal to you. When you get it, you can conclude that for a while she has said goodbye to her scruples.[*]

A parallel tradition of erotic paintings exists in Chinese culture.

[*] There seems to be a certain discrepancy between the urgent infatuation, which, according to Kokkoka, alone justifies the exercise, and this calculating and patient operational approach to seduction: could one of the two, moral precept and practical instruction, possibly be ironic? If so, it is likely to be the moral precept.

CONCERNING COME-HITHER SIGNS

A woman in love does not look you straight in the eye, but becomes confused after a moment and looks away. She manages on various pretexts to let you see her body for a moment. She draws on the ground with her toes. She looks at you surreptitiously and smiles—either from time to time or all the time. If a child is on her knee, she kisses it and talks to it with conspicuous affection. If asked a question she looks down, says something unintelligible and confused, and smiles. On one pretext or another, she hangs about where her man is, talking loudly, in the hope that he will notice her; when she knows he is looking, she carries on an animated conversation as cover. When he appears, she smiles in his direction. She sits on a girlfriend's lap and plays all manner of jokes. She strikes up acquaintances with her servants, plays games, and chats with them; she then asks for news of him. She confides in her friends and talks to them about love. She will not let him see her unadorned; if a friend asks her to make her a garland, she hands it over as if reluctantly. She sighs, looks sideways, beats her breasts with her hand, stifles when talking, taps with her fingers, says ambiguous things and then is embarrassed, yawns, beats the man she loves with flowers, draws an elaborate brow-mark for her friends, touches her hips, opens her eyes wide, lets her hair down, visits the man's house on one pretext after another, sweats from her

While the European tradition was to paint informal poses, Indian aristocrats had their sex lives recorded.

hands and feet, and wipes her brow with her arm—"how many girls has he? how many beauties? which does he like most among them?"—so she questions her intimates privately with deep concern.

OF SEDUCTION—FINAL STAGES

Once she has given you your sign, you can proceed at once to the touching-embrace (sprstaka), and the others in order.

When you bathe together, covertly touch her breasts and buttocks. Give out that you are sick—if she comes to inquire how you fare, seize her hand, ask her to smooth your brow and eyelids, and say to her tenderly, but ambiguously,* "comfort my pain, my lovely —remember it is you who cause it. Surely with all your qualities, o slender one, you won't refuse me this?" Then ask her to undertake some service, such as the pounding of herbs for your medicine.

▲ *A painting from a series recording the love-life of a prince.*

When you give each other betel, flowers, and so forth, touch her lightly with your nails; offer her leaves with significant nail- and toothprints on them.

Finally, get her in a private spot, and there, little by little, enjoy the pleasures of passionate embraces and the rest, and you will pour to the Teacher of Love-Science the repeated libations that your long-nourished desires have stored up.

Women are most inclined to love—and most easily conquered—at night and in pitch darkness. Approached under these conditions, there is hardly a man to whom they can say No. Lastly, for seduction avoid any place inhabited by an old lady who has enjoyed carnal copulation in her time, for where one person has been successfully wooed, it is unlucky to woo a second.†

---

* So that in the event of trouble you could mean only "Please tend my sickness, for the excitement of your visit has made me worse." The Indian lover is hardly rash in his avowals.

† But lucky to build a temple—one function of the maithuna group (see p.15) prescribed by the Acharyas for temple gateways is to guarantee the presence of the good vibrations associated with sex.

This nineteenth-century bazaar copy, while less finely painted than other images, shows unusual intensity.

TESTING HER MIND (Bhavapariksa)

In the course of soliciting a woman, you must try her mind carefully, to see whether she is responding or not. If not, then the teaching is that she will need to be softened by a go-between. If she is responding but is still in two minds, she will come to hand little by little. If she does not openly accept your advances, but nevertheless loiters conspicuously in lonely places, wearing all her ornaments, she is asking to be taken by force. If she accepts an assignation and lets you woo her, she is in love and can be taken of her own free will. If she shrinks from your advances because she is frightened for her own safety but not for yours, you can win her by great gentleness. If she is unwilling but still betrays her love, she will be easily won. If when invited to love she gives a clear answer, she is already conquered, and if she herself makes the advances, she was conquered before you began.

I have given here the detailed rules that apply to women of firm, but not over-bold or forward disposition. I have also made plain how one can tell when a woman has been won.

OF GO-BETWEENS (Dutikarma)

I will now give a short account of the use of go-betweens.* A go-between obtains the ear of the woman by her good character, by offering her magical recipes as a storyteller, and so on. She acquaints the woman with lucky charms and beauty spells from the Veda, medicinal herbs, poetry, and new ways of lovemaking. When she has gained her confidence, the go-between will say to her, "You know, my dear, with your looks, your skill, your intelligence, and your character, you are wasted on such a husband as yours. Oh, how fate has cheated your youthful beauty, which is so averse

---

* There is no one word for duti: I have kept "go-between" though she is not always one in fact. "Bawd" implies prostitution; "seductrix" is as close as one can get.

to everything vulgar and cheap! That jealous, ungrateful, bloodless, double-dealing, and none-too-brainy husband of yours isn't fit to be your footman. What a crying shame!"

By constantly decrying him in these terms, she will implant in the woman seeds of aversion against her husband. Any faults his wife sees in him will automatically be magnified.

When the occasion comes, the go-between will next enlarge on the qualities of the suitor. Once she has awakened interest, she will say, "Listen, my dear—I think you ought to be told. That poor, lovely young fellow is sick. They're afraid for his life. Ever since you looked at him, he has pined—you might as well have been a snake and bitten him— sighing, sweating, falling into a decline, and he never could stand a great deal of sorrow. He says that as the Gods drink nectar from the Moon, so he must drink from your beauty, or he will die. My dear, never even in a dream, has he been so ill!" If this does not seem to disturb the lady, she will at her next visit begin telling her stories of Ahalya* and

others, then about women whose dealings with lovers were accounted virtue in them. Proceeding in this way, she gradually makes her object clear.

By now, your lady jokes with the go-between when she sees her; lets her sit next to her, asks if she has eaten and how she slept, asks her about her news, and generally treats her as an intimate. She sighs, yawns, gives her extra money, asks when the go-

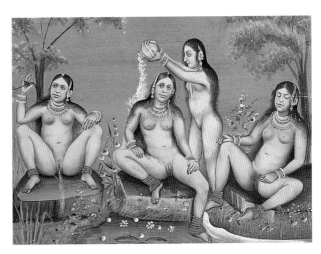

Favorites of the raja's harem these women were relatively fortunate.

between rises to go, "When will you come again?;" she relishes her stories, saying, "How can you tell such scandalous tales when your conversation is so proper? I won't do what you say. I think the fellow is a dissembling rogue." She laughs about his illness and mocks him all the more. If at this stage the go-between has actually conveyed his proposal, the suitor should give her a bonus.

★ Wife of Gautama, seduced by the God Indra.

The go-between will continue to ply the lady with gifts of betel, flowers, and perfume. Once she has made her thoroughly enamored, she will arrange for the pair to meet accidentally, taking advantage of a family disaster, a wedding, or a festival; or else in a park, at a drinking-party, at a procession, when bathing, when a fire breaks out, when some emergency threatens, or in the go-between's own house.

VARIETIES OF GO-BETWEEN (*duti*)

A go-between who understands her principal's intention, manages the whole affair, and sees it to completion is known as nisrstartha [a *chargée d'affaires*].

A go-between who only takes the matter to the point of getting some response, but does not finish the business, is parimatartha [a limited negotiator].

One who merely carries messages between lovers is patrahari [a letter carrier].

One who ostensibly acts as agent of a lover, but is actually in business on her own account and promoting schemes of her own, is called svayamduti [a private operator].* She may pose as an innocent, gain the confidence of a man's wife, but secretly learn from her all her husband's secrets and seduce him for herself. Such is a (mugdha)† duti.

A lover can employ his own wife as an unwitting go-between if he introduces her to his mistress, knowing she will boast of his sexual skill. Such a wife-go-between is called bharyaduti.

---

* Either she will seduce the seducer for herself, or she will be a procuress acting as a two-way go-between, first upsetting a married woman, then finding her a lover.

† Mugdha ("trembling"): a young girl with no sex experience, as opposed to praudha, a mature woman; here a separate category of duti. According to Vatsyayana, she sows every sort of dissension between husband and wife, making ostentatious nailmarks on herself and for the wife to see. This type of duti is perhaps the only one commonly extant in our own culture.

One Indian translation I have seen makes the duti or paid go-between a double agent—employed by the seducer to get around his mistress, but in fact bribed by the seducer's wife to drop hints, behave tactlessly, and in every conceivable way betray the whole plot to the aggrieved husband.

◄ *A painting showing a prince with members of his harem.*

One can send a young girl, or a nun, who knows none of the tricks of the trade, to smuggle a love-letter in a garland or an ear ornament. A young girl who has no idea what is afoot and who carries letters hidden in jewelry or leaves with nail- and toothmarks on them is called a "dumb" go-between (mukaduti).

A "dumb" go-between who carries messages with a double meaning, previously agreed signs, or private allusions not generally comprehensible, is called a wind-go-between (vataduti): in this case the lady can send a reply without fear of detection.

Reliable go-betweens are: slave-girls, friends of the lady, young girls, wise-women, widows, artists, garland-sellers, perfumers, wives of laundrymen, begging nuns, peddler-women, nurses and neighbors.* Men of the world also use parrots and mynahs, as well as pictures, for purposes of seduction.

Some lovers, who have employed slave-girls to reconnoiter for them, actually force their way into other men's harems. This practice brings reprobation both in this world and the next, and I will pass over it in silence.

★ All of them female.

NOTE ON THE TRANSLATION

I would like to be franker than some past "translators" of Sanskrit about the scholarly claims of this version. My knowledge of the language is confined to what little I have acquired in studying this literature for its content, and without existing translations into other languages I could not have made much of the Koka Shastra. All work on Sanskrit erotica owes more or less of its matter (in my case, more) to Richard Schmidt's great scholarly compendium of Sanskrit texts with translations, partly into German and partly into Latin (1911), and to his German edition of the Kama Sutra and Jayamangala; I also had Leinhard's full and authoritative German translation of the Koka Shastra, Iyengar's translation of the Kama Sutra, the help of Indian friends, and the various other English and Indian versions of Sanskrit erotica already mentioned. On the other hand, I have not simply translated a translation—I have been through the original text and the translations not with any hope of poaching successfully on Sanskrit scholarship, but to see how far I could make sense of them in terms of what is now known of sexual behavior in other cultures, and of human biology generally. Sanskrit scholars will probably be wise to ignore this version altogether, as a paraphrase, and go to Leinhard, if not to the original. For reasons I have given in the Introduction, it is the scientific audience and the general public I really had in mind.

Further Reading

Al-Nefzawi (Umar Ibn Muhammad), *The Perfumed Garden*, translated by Sir Richard Burton, (London: Hamlyn, 1989)

Anand, M. R., *Kama Kalia*, (London: Skilton, 1958)

Basham, A. L., *The Wonder that was India*, (London: Sigwick & Jackson, 1954)

Basu, B. N., *The Kama Sutra of Vatsyayana*, revised by S. L. Ghosh. Tenth edition, (Calcutta: Medical Book Co, 1951)

Brown, W. N., *The Vasanta Vilasa*, (New Haven: American Oriental Society (Illustrated), 1962)

Chandra, P., *The Kaula-Kapalika Cults at Khajuraho*, Lalit Kala, 1–2, 98–197, (1955)

Comfort, A., *Darwin and the Naked Lady*, (London: Routledge & Kegan Paul, 1961)

De, S. K., *Ancient Indian Erotics and Erotic Literature*, (Calcutta: Mukhopadyay, 1959)

Dickinson, R. L., *Human Sex Anatomy*, (Baltimore: Williams & Wilkins, 1933)

Egerton, C., (translation), *The Golden Lotus—Chin P'ing Mei*, (London: Routledge & Kegan Paul, 1939)

Eliade, M., *Yoga: Immortality and Freedom*, (London: Routledge & Kegan Paul, 1958)

Ford, C. S. and Beach, F. A., *Patterns of Sexual Behavior*, (London: Practitioner, 1952)

Forman, H., *Through Forbidden Tibet*, (London: Jarrolds, 1936)

Goetz, H., *The Historical Background of the Great Temples at Khajuraho*, (Arts Asiat. Paris, 5 (i), 1958)

Gulik, R. H. van, *Erotic Color Prints of the Ming Period with an Essay on Chinese Sex Life from the Han to the Ch'ing Dynasty*, 3 volumes, (Privately Printed, 1951)

Ibid, *Sexual Life in Ancient China*, (Leiden: Brill, 1961)

Rangaswami Iyengar, K., *The Kama Sutra of Vatsyayana*, (Lahore: Punjab Skr. Book Depot, 1921)

Kalyana-malla, *Ananga-Ranga*, edited by Visnu-prasada Bhandari, (Kashi Sanskrit Series No 9), (Benmares, 1923)

Kalyana-malla, *Ananga-Ranga*, translated by Sir Richard Burton and F. F. Arbuthnot, (Cosmopoli: Kama Shastra Society, 1885)

Kannoomal, *Some Notes on Hindu Erotics*, Rupam, 4, 20–7 (1920)

Kokkoka, *Rati-rahasyam: Srimat-Kancinatha-krta-Dipikakhyaya vyakhyaya samudbhasitam*, edited by Ghildiyal, (Lahore: Bombay Sanskrit Press, 1923)

Kokkoka, *Rati-rahasyam: Devidatta Sarmana tippanikaya visadikrtya sodhitam*, (Benares: Tara Press, 1912)

Krishna Deva, *The Temple of Khajuraho in Central India*, Ancient India, 15, 43–65, (1959)

Leinhard, S., *Kokkoka-Ratirahasya*, (Stuttgart: Vranz Decker, 1960)

Maspero, H., *Procedes de 'nourrir le principe vital' dans la Religion Taoiste Ancienne*, J. Asiat, 229, 177–353, (1937)

Meyer, J. J., *Sexual Life in Ancient India*, 2 volumes, (Delhi: Motilal Barnarsidas, 1971)

Muttumanitalam, M. C., *Kokkokasastram*, Allepy. Vidyarambham, (1959)

Nagarasarvasra of Padmasri, edited by Tansakhram Sarma, (Bombay: Gujrati Press, 1921)

Nagarjuna Siddha, *Ratisastra*, translated by A. C. Ghose, (Calcutta: Seal, 1904)

Narayana Prasada Misra, Koka-sara-vaidyaka, (1937)

Panigrahi, K. C., *Obscene Sculpture of Orissan Temples*, Proc Ind Hist Congr 8, 94–7, (1945)

Panigrahi, K. C., *Archaeological Remains at Bhubaneswar*, (Bombay Orient: Longmans, 1961)

Pandit, M. P., *Lights on the Tantra*, (Madras: Ganesh, 1957)

Pavolini, S., *Ratimanjari of Jayadeva*, Giorn Soc Asiat Ital 17, 317, (1904)

Pisani, V., *Storia delle Letterature Antiche Dell-India*, (Milan: Nuovo Acad Editrice, 1954)

Ramakrishna Gopala Bhandarkar (Sir), Vaisnavism, *Saivism and Minor Religious Systems*, Grundr Indoasichen Philologie u Alterstumskunde. Band II, Heft 6, (Tuber: Strassburg, 1913)

Anon, *Rati-sastra-ratnavali—Hindu Sexual Science*, (Madras, 1905)

Ratiratnapradipika of Maharaja Devaraja, edited by Liladhur Sarma, (Calcutta: Benkateswar Book Agency, 1930).

Rawson, P., *Erotic Art of India*, (London: Thames & Hudson, 1977)

Ray, T. L., translated, *Kokkokam and Ratirahasyam*, (Calcutta: Medical Book Agency, 1960)

Ray, T. L., translated, *Ananga-Ranga*, (Calcutta: Medical Book Agency, 1944)

Schmidt, R., *Beitrage zur Indischen Erotik: Das Liebesleben des Sanskritvolkes*, (Berlin: Barsdorf, 1922)

Schmidt, R., *Das Kama-Sutram des Vatsyayana*, (Berlin: Barsdorf, 1907)

Schmidt, R, *Hariharas Srngaradipika*, Zeit. Deutsches Morg. Ges., 57, 705–39, (1903)

Schmidt, R, *Das Ratisastra des Nagarjuna*, Weiner Z f Kult. Morgenland, 23, 180–90, (1909)

Sinha, I., *Tantra, The Search for Ecstasy*, (London: Hamlyn, 1993)

Sivaramamurti, C., *Sanskrit Literature and Art—Mirrors of Indian Art and Culture*, Mem Arch survey, India. No 73, (1955)

Spate, O. H. K., *Konarak & Sindri: Fertility Ancient and Modern*, Meanjin Pap. 1957 (4), 341–53, (1957)

Totajaya, Y., *The Kokkokam of Ativira Rama Pandian*, (Calcutta: Medical Book Co, 1949)

Upadhyaya, S. C., *Studies in Ancient Indian Erotics*, J. Gujarat Res Soc 15 (1953)

van Weck-Erlen, L. (Weckerle, J pseud), *Das goldne Buch der Liebe*, 2 volumes. (Vienna: p.p, 1907)

Vatsyayana: *Kama Sutra*, translated by S. C. Upadhyaya, (London: Chas. Skilton, 1963)

Vatsyayana: *Kama Sutra*, translated by Sir Richard Burton and F. F. Arbuthnot, with a preface by W. G. Archer, (London: George Allen & Unwin, 1963)

Wood, E., *Yoga*, (London: Penguin, 1959)

Zannas, E. and Auboyer, J., *Khzajuraho*, (The Hague: Mouton, 1960)